And Yet, I Still Loved France

Connie Colker Steiner   Renée Kann Silver

Published by Marble House Editions

96-09 66th Avenue (Suite 1D)

Rego Park, NY 11374

www.marble-house-editions.com

Library of Congress Cataloguing-in-Publication Data

Colker Steiner, Connie and Kann Silver, Renée

And Yet, I Still Loved France

Summary: The memoir of a European Jewish woman who recalls her World War II childhood in France.

ISBN 978-0-9834030-2-9

Library of Congress Catalog Card Number 2011944092

Printed in China

"People who agonize don't act; people who act don't agonize."

-Pierre Sauvage in an interview with Bill Moyers about his documentary Weapons of the Spirit, 1990.

Dedicated to the memories of

Pasteur Trocmé of Le Chambon sur Lignon,
Monsieur et Madame Caussidière of Villeurbanne.

Without their help, my parents, my sister Edith, and I could not have survived the year 1942 in Vichy France.

Acknowledgements

Ein Hitler Schicksal is a memoir my father wrote to document the events affecting my family with the arrival of Hitler in the Saarland. I have referred to it to ascertain exact dates of the events that shaped our lives from 1935 until 1947. It is a document I translated from the German into English, and I still marvel at my father's total absence of bitterness and his constant ability to see goodness in people. Despite his own handicap, my father was ever concerned for others who suffered and ready to help.

~ Renée Kann Silver

* * *

I would like to express gratitude to the Jewish Foundation of Manitoba for supporting this project in its early stages.

Thanks also to my husband, Mark, my "first editor," for his careful reading, encouragement, and patience with the time required to develop the book.

A special appreciation to my co-author, Renée, who allowed me to accompany her as she revisited the beauty and terror of her childhood.

~ Connie Colker Steiner

Part One

If A Bomb Hits You,

Lie Down Flat

1931 – 1942

English Channel (La Manche)

Saarbrücken

Sarreguemines

Bar-le-duc
Longeville en Barrois

Paris

Vichy

Basel

Villeurbanne • Annecy
Lyon
St. Etienne

Le Chambon
sur Lignon

Atlantic
Ocean

Gurs

Marseille

Mediterranean

...... Demarcation line
betwee Occupied
and Non Occupied (Vichy) France

Chapter 1

I stood, arms folded behind my back. All the children did the same, as we were trained by our teachers. It was best for posture, they said. We were gathered in the courtyard of the Ecole Anatole France, an elementary school for girls in Villeurbanne, a town bordering the city of Lyon. The year was 1942. I was eleven.

We were arranged by class and, two by two, we formed perfect lines. Across the yard, with the younger students, was my little sister. Our age difference wasn't great. She was nine. But Edith depended on me a lot, and that made me feel older. Nearby, with her class, was my best friend. We shared first names - Renée. Renée and Renée, the two Renées. The thought made me smile. Above us was a glass ceiling so foggy with dust it hid the sky. The sky itself was gray, and the air hung warm and humid at the end of June. But my spirits didn't match the weather. I liked being there with my friends and teachers all around. It was fun coming outside, breaking the usual routine. Why we were assembled I didn't know. They never told us in advance.

The *Directrice*, Madame de C., stepped before us and spoke. "Our great leader has asked us to select a student for her excellence in studies, classroom behavior, athletic ability and sportsmanship."

Our great leader. Madame de C. was talking about the *Maréchal*, the leader of our part of France. To us he was France. Portraits of his grandfatherly face gazed down as we walked in the hallways. We raised the flag and saluted him with songs at least once a week. We brought money from home that the school collected and sent to him. We wrote letters to him about how we loved him, and how well things were going. And he sent encouraging letters to us. It was true he didn't actually write them, but we still looked forward to getting them, and seeing his official-looking stamped signature. Our school was named after Anatole France, a famous writer. But it could easily have been called the Ecole Maréchal Pétain.

I didn't know then that he had brought France close to Hitler's Nazi Germany and Mussolini's Fascist Italy. I didn't know that the ideas and actions of the men around him would bring misery to people like me and my family. To us at the Ecole Anatole France he was a hero. Every girl adored him - I as much as the next.

Madame de C. continued, "This is a very special honor and the Maréchal has generously donated a book about his life to be awarded to the winner." She took a deep breath. "Although Renée Kann has been chosen, I am certain the Maréchal would not want his prize to go to anyone of her race. France has been caused too many problems by this race already. The prize will go instead to Monique ..."

I heard nothing more. My straight posture crumpled. My hands reached for my apron and my face came down to meet it. I felt everyone's eyes, everyone's combined curiosity. I heard the footsteps of two teachers as they approached and put their arms around me. Their sympathy, which called more attention to me, made everything worse. I buried my head. My shoulders shook with silent sobs. But even in shock and confusion I couldn't help wondering: why didn't they simply hand the prize to the other girl? Why was I held up as someone vile? There must be some crime, some stain that I carried. Madame de C. said I had harmed my country. What could I have done? I loved this land. When I said my nighttime prayer and asked God to look after Maman and Papa and Edith and *Grandpère*, I never forgot to ask His blessing for France, my beautiful country.

Arms still crossed to hide my face, I managed to leave the assembly and return to class. I picked up my books and slate and waited for Edith. Then the two of us walked back to the apartment.

Chapter 2

Villeurbanne was not my first home. I was born in
Saarbrücken, capital of the Saarland. Saarbrücken means
"bridge crossing the Saar" - the river that gave the city and the
whole region its name. The Saarland was a place that France
and Germany argued and sometimes fought over. It went back
and forth between the two countries. After World War I ended
in 1918, there was an agreement that the Saarland would, for
a period of time, belong to neither. That's how it was - just
itself - when I started life in 1931.

Being very small, I knew nothing of countries and borders.
There were me and Mami and Papa on the third floor of a fine
apartment house. The top floor was set aside for the maids
who worked in the building. On the floor below us were
the Schaeffers. They had two little girls. Mami or Grete, the
maid we loved and trusted, sometimes took me to see them.
I would walk carefully down the stairs, remembering to be
quiet, remembering my manners. The Schaeffer girls - with
their mother or nanny - visited us. Everyone in the building
shared a garden which was divided into sections, one to a
family. Papa had transformed our bit of green into a rock
garden. He puttered there on Sundays. I would watch, my
fingers exploring the varied surfaces of the stones.

My friend Margarete lived in a house on the other side of the
garden. We were the same age. I called her Margaretchen. She
would join me and Mami for strolls in the forest near our

home. Or it might be Grete who walked with us among the trees, on soft ground covered with pine needles. We breathed sweet smells of soil and resin. After rain the perfume was stronger. I enjoyed our rock garden but this forest was even better. To me it was an enchanted land inhabited by fairytale characters. Margaretchen shared my feelings.

Nothing stays the same. Grete moved away to get married. My baby sister Edith arrived, and another young woman was brought in to help Mami. Else was devoted to the baby but didn't want my friends tagging along on walks. I played with Margaretchen at home in the garden. Sometimes she and her mother invited me to go with them to the forest. Once there, we checked under the mushrooms for dwarves, gathered red berries that to us were tiny creatures, and stared up at trees that rose far above our heads. We imagined they were giants.

In fairytales there are dangers. Enchanted woods can hold ogres, trolls, wicked witches - often wearing pleasant disguises. If I thought about these things at all, I was never afraid. The forest, with its strange light, scented air and mysterious rustling sounds, always seemed welcoming.

The real world had its dangers too. Sorting friend from foe was becoming confusing. There was the day Herr Schaeffer appeared in a curious brown uniform. Suddenly Mami said I mustn't play with the children downstairs, not in their apartment and not in ours. She didn't explain why and I didn't ask. My parents looked worried now, and this troubled me.

It wasn't getting better with my new nanny. No warm connection was developing - nothing like the closeness I had felt for Grete. Else clearly loved baby Edith best. When the three of us went out, she wheeled the carriage fast, pulling me hard by the hand. Maybe she didn't like being slowed down. I felt like extra baggage.

But once she took me on an adventure, which in my eyes meant she liked me at least a little. We went downtown. The buildings must have been empty, I thought, because everyone was outside. Tall, handsome, uniformed men stood lining the parade. Else put me on the shoulders of one of the young men so I could see. I held on to his head, laughing. A parade was coming closer. The crowd was cheering a man in uniform with a moustache, standing in an open car. He saluted, his arm straight out. The cheering got louder. I looked up at the red, white and black banners hanging everywhere, fluttering smartly in the breeze. They had an odd symbol on them, like a black "X" with broken arms.

We came home. I saw that in my neighborhood there were banners hanging from the windows just like the ones downtown. Why didn't we have one too? Night fell. Fat candles in glass holders gleamed from the outside windowsills of every apartment but ours. Rows of tiny flames flickered like stars. The banners, catching their glow, could be seen against the dark. Never had a day been so exciting, or an evening so beautiful. Why weren't we also celebrating?

Mami and Papa were terrible killjoys. They refused to participate and seemed determined to squash my happiness.

Else, who had for once done something fun with me, got no thanks from them either. Mami and Papa were angry with her for our little trip downtown!

I didn't understand their reasons. Why didn't they want me among people cheering Adolph Hitler - whoever that was? What was wrong with sitting on the shoulders of an SS officer? Only my parents knew. They seemed very sure of their opinions.

Despite her mistake, Else was allowed to stay on with us. There were no more parades for me. That didn't mean Else stopped admiring the Nazis. Along with our laundry she began washing the uniforms of the boys in the Hitler Youth. My parents discovered this and Else quickly disappeared from my life.

Soon we would be leaving too.

In 1935 the population of the Saarland had to decide which country to join. As always, the choice was between Germany and France. By a great majority the people chose Germany, now ruled by Hitler.

Mami and Papa knew we could not stay. The danger was too great. My parents said goodbye to their friends - that is, to those of their friends who had not become Nazis. Papa had to say goodbye to the men he employed. Most of them loved him. Even, it seemed, those who had joined the Nazi Party. For me, there was no point in saying anything to the children downstairs. The Schaeffer girls had long stopped speaking to me. But I hated to leave Margaretchen and the forest walks. Her family never accepted Nazism. Nothing came between her and me. Besides, the year before, I had cut her hair according to my notions of style. The results were alarming. If that didn't wreck our friendship, nothing would. And so, at the age of four, I left Saarbrücken, together with Papa and Mami, and Edith who understood even less of this than I.

Chapter 3

"Mon Dieu!" cried Denise's mother. She raced from the house
to the road. Her geese had waddled to the other side, as was
their habit. While they were gone men had come and put
down a coat of tar. Maman and Papa Goose and their goslings
were caught on the return trip. Unable to move, they set up a
noisy appeal for rescue.

My friend Denise and I were playing beside the house, near
her father's woodworking shop. Her younger brother, just
beyond babyhood, was with us. We ran to see better what
was happening. At first all we could do was watch as Denise's
mother fetched each bird, cradling it in her apron for the
journey to the kitchen. When the flock was safe, the *maman*
and *papa* had their webbed feet cleaned. They were sent,
protesting, to the yard, so we could turn our attention to
the goslings.

Denise's mother used butter to wipe tar from the squirming
little shapes. She finished by washing them with water.
Denise's brother, too young for any task, looked on seriously.
We, the four-year-olds, were trusted to take a big towel and
carefully pat down the goslings. Finally, after a brief warm-up
near the wood-burning stove, they emerged fluffy and dry, no
worse for their experience. Throughout our labors, squawks
from outdoors invaded the kitchen. The two parents were
objecting loudly and continuously to their banishment.

Sitting with a gosling in my lap, feeling its small heart beat, was a far distance from streetcars and apartments. Saarbrücken, even with a forest nearby, was a city. Now I lived in a valley of Alsace, France. Instead of the River Saar, my new village, Diemeringen, was built around a brook whose name I never knew. Most of the houses were farmhouses, some with just a few chickens, others real working farms. Only the newest houses had running water. Ours wasn't finished when we moved in. We had to wait for indoor plumbing. The houses faced the one main street. Farmers piled manure and straw shoveled from the stables in front of their homes, toward the road. These heaps, called *fumiers*, fermented, turning gradually into fertilizer. Most of the windows in the houses were in the back, looking out on more agreeable views of fields, gardens and fruit trees.

In the center of town was a small public square bordered by a church, a hall for the mayor and other officials called the *mairie*, two shops, a café, a hair salon and dentist's office. Sometimes tables crammed with things to buy lined the square. When the traveling fair arrived it spread from the square into the side streets with food, dancing, a musical band and game stalls. But these events were rare. Usually the square was empty. What Diemeringen had in large supply were meadows.

I could pick the forget-me-nots that grew near the brook and collect tiny daisies, the *pâquerettes* that in April turned whole fields white. I had friends - Denise, Jacqueline and Nicole. They taught me to make crowns and necklaces from the *pâquerettes.* I would slit a stem with my fingernail and push another stem through. Then I'd pull until it was stopped by the bright petalled head of the flower. We did the same with yellow primroses. It was easier since they were bigger and had thicker stems.

The flowers grew wild. Anybody could grab a bunch. The rules and restraints of Saarbrücken fell away and I could run and shout as I pleased. No nanny yanked me by the hand. Grownup eyes didn't follow my adventures or hedge my decisions. Maman was busy tending my sister, who was often sick. Papa commuted so long to his business that we only saw him on weekends. Maman was left to pump water and heat it for our baths, tend the vegetable garden, walk to the farms to fill her net bag with eggs, butter and milk. I liked to stay with her and help - or think I was helping. But many days I was off on my own, roaming with my friends. She was probably glad I didn't need much attention.

In Diemeringen I really didn't. I turned up alone to meet Maman at the beauty salon. No one accompanied me to the dentist. Sometimes I went without any appointment, just to say *bonjour* and prove my independence. More and more I was speaking French rather than the German I had learned in Saarbrücken. Diemeringen was in the province of Alsace, so people understood German too. I grew into my new language with little effort.

The fair came to town and Jacqueline and I went together. Like Denise, she was my age. We didn't invite any grown-ups. Even though men got drunk, and certain target games involved the use of real guns, we knew what to do and what to avoid. Jacqueline loved to dance. She managed to get me on a wooden platform among adult couples who were stepping in time to music. While a band played we tried to pick up the "fox trot." Jacqueline had some success, but I was relieved when we left off dancing. The games offered superior possibilities, I thought.

We found a booth away from the noise of guns shooting at decoy ducks. It was perfect. We threw fabric-covered balls at tin cans arranged on shelves. At the end of the rounds I won the right to select a prize. A small plaster statue of a lady caught my attention. She was white like marble. Her eyes looked down. She had a tender, calm smile and her hands were clasped in prayer. She looked like an angel. I knew adults thought highly of these statues. My *grandpère* sold such "ladies" in his decorating shop. I had seen his customers buying them and heard Maman say they were lovely. Now she could own one! I hurried home to present her with my treasure.

She wouldn't keep it. It was a Madonna, she said. It had no place in a Jewish household. I took the beautiful Madonna statue back to the fair. The man let me choose another gift. I brought home two goldfish swimming in a glass bowl.

I didn't think much about religion, then. We had Hanukkah and Passover instead of Christmas and Easter. We celebrated Hanukkah quietly at home and shared a bit of Christmas when we visited neighbors and admired their decorations. We weren't the only Jews in Diemeringen. I remember being invited to a Passover Seder. There was a synagogue off the square, down one of the side streets, which Papa attended on Saturday mornings. When he asked me I went with him. Other fathers brought their children too. The men would be standing, holding books and reading softly, each at his own pace. I couldn't understand what they were saying. Papa told me it was Hebrew, a language for talking to God. I heard a kind of mumbling, wall to wall. Sometimes the words came together in chanting or song, which was better. I liked especially to hear the voice of the prayer leader rise above the rest and continue alone, filling the room with sweet, mysterious sounds. He was the cantor, Papa said. His melodies had to carry everyone's prayer to heaven.

On that day, the Sabbath, we weren't permitted to write, draw, sew or even pick flowers. We followed the Jewish dietary laws, though we weren't strict. Maman never served milk and meat together. Some foods she didn't serve at all - like pork, or *escargots*, the snails that crawled in the meadow. I loved to hunt for them. When the grass was wet with dew or rain they were easy to find. The perfect shape of their houses fascinated me. Brown, beige and pink, the spirals went round and round and seemed to have no beginning or end. How did the creatures get in and out? One day I collected enough to fill a bucket. Maman wouldn't be interested, I knew. I took them to the Schmidts, a family that had three handsome sons and, every Christmas, a large tree with real clip-on candles. Monsieur Schmidt gave me two francs for my catch.

15

What fascinated me more than religious differences were the distinctions - new to me - between boys and girls.

Boys and girls, men and women, wore different clothing and had their hair cut at different lengths. Men could grow hair on their faces, and had lower voices. Beyond this, I assumed much was the same. My parents had always been careful not to undress in front of me. The baby in our house was a girl like me. But my friend Denise (of the goslings) had a brother about two years old.

He and I and Denise would play outside between her house and the carpentry shop. We made flower chains and crowns for him. He was like a little toy, better than dolls. His mother would check on us from the kitchen window, and rescue him if our games got out of bounds. He had what I considered an astonishing talent. Whenever he felt the need, he watered the grass where he stood. Using a part of the body that I didn't have and had never seen, he sent a stream straight out in front of him.

I observed that grown men possessed the same talent, particularly when the fair was on and they staggered from too much wine or beer. They urinated against stone walls and against the farmers' compost heaps of manure and straw.

Short hair for boys, longer hair for girls, I was beginning to realize, hinted at something more complicated. I didn't suspect a link with babies and how they got here. At four, I presumed a stork brought them. Nobody told me. My parents were silent on the subject. But it was obvious. I had only to look at birth announcements. They all displayed drawings of this particular large bird carrying a sack with a baby inside. A pair of storks actually did migrate to Diemeringen every year. They nested on the roof of the midwife's house, in her chimney. As I understood it, a woman went to the midwife and waited. When the time was right, a stork brought the baby down from the chimney - delivered it!

Then something happened to challenge my ideas, to make me draw a new conclusion.

I was with my third friend, Nicole. I liked to visit her because her father was a potter and I could watch him turn clay on a wheel. Also, they had a farm with more than chickens and geese. They had pigs and cows, and sometimes piglets and calves. The piglets arrived in bunches. I didn't see them as anything like human babies. But once I witnessed the birth of a calf.

It came alone - just one - like infants come. I knew at once and finally that storks had nothing to do with it. I watched how tenderly the parent animal cared for its little one, licking and nuzzling it. My thoughts wandered to how I liked cuddling with my own parents, especially early on weekend mornings, when my father was home.

The very next Saturday morning I climbed into their bed, on my father's side. I had something to say.

"I bet you don't know that I know where babies really come from!"

Silence.

"It's not the stork."

"*Non?*"

"*Non!*"

"Where then?" they asked.

"Your belly!" I laughed and poked my father in the stomach.

I knew it came from a parent's belly. Eventually I would know which one. Neither of mine told me the truth that morning.

Little was imposed on me, the two years I spent in Diemeringen. Except for the rhythms of nature, the routines of home, the needs of my body, I was free. I hadn't entered school yet. I was four and five, and the meadow and village and farms were my classroom. I was always learning. My discoveries delighted me.

I wasn't aware of things I would have found disturbing. There was the cow in the pasture and the roast on the table. I didn't relate one to the other. I had no idea Denise's goslings would someday be force-fed and served as liver pâté. I didn't know what people did to animals. I didn't know, didn't imagine, what people could do to each other.

Chapter 4

I remember little about the day we moved. Did we take a train or go by car? If by car, who drove? Was it Maman, or was it Papa's chauffeur? One thing is certain. It wasn't Papa. My father had fought in the First World War, barely surviving a gunshot wound to the head. Though he recovered, the right side of his brain was injured, affecting the left side of his body. He dragged his left leg. His left arm was frozen against his side, the hand unable to straighten. If he fell he couldn't break the fall. Often he struggled with slow-healing broken ribs. He was prone to something like epileptic seizures, which worsened if he became upset. He depended on his chauffeur, who handled a variety of tasks, not just driving. And he depended on my mother.

It was probably Maman behind the wheel that day. She was always there, helping him. They shared a great love. She admired his tenacity, the will that enabled him to successfully run his own scrap metal business. And Papa couldn't believe his luck. A beautiful woman had accepted him despite his handicap. Maman had thick chestnut hair, a warm smile, impishly tipped nose and lively gray-green eyes. One more green than gray. The other more gray than green. People didn't see the difference unless they were told. Maman was small – not much more than five feet – but sturdy. She had strong arms that could lift and carry and do everything. She was very feminine and enjoyed pretty clothes. A seamstress made the silk or cotton dresses that skimmed her figure. I didn't think of her as beautiful but as I grew I realized that others did. The feelings my parents had for each other expanded easily to include us children. Papa hadn't dared dream he would have any. Edith and I filled him with pride. He took seriously our every small achievement.

A scrap metal yard depends directly on the needs of steel mills. When I was born, Papa's business sold scrap to the mills in the Saarland and the Ruhr. Now Papa was based in Sarreguemines, on the other side of the Saar River spelled differently, the French way. When we first moved to France - to Diemeringen - it was to Sarreguemines that he commuted. He spent the week there, returning to us on Fridays. Diemeringen was in the province of Alsace. Sarreguemines, to the north, was in Lorraine. After two years, we were finally living near Papa's work. Why we didn't do this in the first place has never been explained to me.

Sarreguemines, France and Saarbrücken, Germany were seventeen kilometers apart, about ten miles. In places, the river formed a natural border between the two countries. It wasn't especially wide. A swimmer of no distinction could cross it, starting out in one country and finishing up in the other. It was all really the Saarland, that mixture of people and dialects straddling two nations, divided between them, often claimed by both, an excuse for too many wars.

Once settled in Sarreguemines, we managed some visits with our relatives across the river. (Only Papa, Maman, Edith and I had fled when Hitler came to power. Our grandparents, aunts, uncles and cousins remained behind in what was now Nazi Germany.) The physical distance between us and the rest of the family was small. But getting together would become increasingly difficult because of the stricter rules for travel between France and Germany. The border guards soon demanded special permits.

My cousins were on Papa's side of the family. Jules and Kurt lived in Saarbrücken. Though much older, they treated me well and I liked them. Their parents, Uncle Nathan (Papa's brother) and Aunt Berthe, had taken care of me when Edith was born. Having no girls of their own, they fussed over us. Aunt Gusta (Papa's sister) and Uncle Ernst lived in a small town an hour from the city. Their children were cousins Leon and Lucie. Leon was eleven and already a teenager. He told coarse jokes and couldn't pass a lingerie shop without comment. His fifteen year-old sister Lucie was better company. When I visited her house she taught me to ride a bicycle. They lived near our grandmother (Papa's mother). We called her "Oma," a German word. She was demanding and domineering. Though devoted to her children and grandchildren, she regarded more critically those who had merely married into the family. Maman didn't enjoy our visits with her. I could tell. I had to contain my annoyance when Oma directed a sharpened word toward my mother. I couldn't imagine anyone finding fault with Maman. I knew how fiercely she loved Papa, how she understood and protected him, often doing the work of two. They were happy together. Couldn't Oma see that? Oma approved of me, and I loved her as part of the family, but I didn't exactly like her. I overheard a discussion between Maman and Aunt Berthe. When Aunt Berthe called

Oma "the Dragon," I silently agreed.

Opa - my grandfather - and my other Oma were Maman's parents. They lived in the town of Zülpich, an hour or two from Saarbrücken. This Oma was a quiet elegant lady. She loved us, we knew. But she was not given to - nor did we expect - hugs and displays of emotion. For that we could count on warm, outgoing Opa. Maman was close to him, and through her I caught the feeling. My mother had two brothers and a younger sister but was the only one to marry and have children. So Edith and I captured all the affections grandparents reserve for their grandchildren.

Opa ran a decorating business. There was a store in front of their house where he sold wallpaper, paints and moldings. Behind the house on one side was a workshop, on the other side a shed where he cut glass for windows, mirrors, picture frames and tabletops. A cobblestone yard covered the area between the shop, the house and the garden. Almost the entire yard was roofed over by a grapevine. Best of all, from my point of view, was the large garden beside the house. My sandbox was in the back, in front of a stone wall that rose to the height of a tall man. Near the sandbox was a walk-in dollhouse, complete with electric lighting.

My grandparents had a dog and cat. Even after my long absence, Dobbie and Hex hadn't forgotten me. Hex, the cat, had a litter which I was anxious to mother. I liked to put her kittens in a toy carriage and wheel them into the dollhouse. Hex didn't really appreciate my efforts. Perhaps she was hiding them from me when she transported them, one kitten at a time, from a third story window to the branches of the towering Bing cherry tree. She needed help getting them down.

Opa loved music, art and architecture, and infected everyone with his enthusiasm. When he examined great country houses in order to plan their decoration, he took note of the surroundings. He returned to paint and draw outdoors in watercolor and pen and ink. He took me on forest walks, turning over rocks with his walking stick to reveal the surprising life underneath. These walks started early, when I was a baby in Saarbrücken. All my forest walks to come, my delight in trees and clouds and growing things, were echoes of these first experiences.

Opa enjoyed people as much as nature and art. His house faced the main street, where everything important in Zülpich happened. Before we moved away to Diemeringen I remember standing at Opa's doorstep, looking out. I was three years old. I watched a procession of little girls dressed in white, on their way to first communion at the nearby Catholic church. Opa was with me. He probably knew the families as he was on friendly terms with everyone, Jew and Christian. I noticed that very small girls my own age walked before the older girls, and from ribboned baskets strewed flower petals to the left and right. The petals seemed in no hurry to reach their destinations. They floated, gently touching ground. I was fascinated and envious. I spent the rest of that visit gathering horse chestnuts, throwing them into the sandbox. Some sprouted and three years later had grown into little trees.

Chapter 5

The apartment we rented in Sarreguemines was very like our first one in Saarbrücken. Even the maid, Sophie, lived on a top floor set aside for household help, just as Grete and Else had done. Sophie came from the countryside near Diemeringen. She was only fifteen, the same age as my cousin Lucie, almost a friend for Edith and me. Soon, though, I would be stepping into a world independent of parents, sister, relatives, nanny. The time had come for me to enter *l'école primaire*, primary school.

On my first day, Maman took me to a photography studio. I was wearing a soft fitted coat, had a knapsack on my back and a jaunty beret angled over a short bob. (A color snapshot would have revealed the red hair with which I quickly became identified.) My father carried this picture in his wallet for the rest of his life.

At school we began at once learning numbers and letters. We learned how to write in longhand without ever being taught to print. We worked on slates. Each slate was framed in wood and had a place to attach a rag for erasing. We wrote with special chalk. It was narrow as a pencil and covered with paper that we peeled back as the chalk wore down. On one side of the slate were lines. They were a centimeter apart - about half an inch, made for practicing over and over numbers and letters, those mysterious figures that held the keys to all future knowledge. Only when our work was perfect did we commit it to paper. Then we dipped our wooden pens with their metal nibs into the inkwells that were set into our desks. The ink was purple. From grade one until high school graduation we were offered only this color which I supposed was the color of all inks. To help us form our letters exactly, the paper we used was ruled in sets of five lines. When it came to the top of an "h," the tail of an "f," the crossing of a "t," nothing was left to chance. Like purple ink, this type of lined paper accompanied us through all the school years, encouraging careful writing at every age. We always wore aprons to protect our dresses from ink stains.

There was no subject called patriotism. There didn't have to be. Love of country found its way into everything like an invisible but very active ingredient. We thrilled to tales of knights and kings and a brave peasant girl named Jeanne d'Arc who saved France from the English invaders during something called the Hundred Years War. She was betrayed by the Burgundians and burned as a witch. That was history - the parts that made for good stories – served up in small portions for our young age. Jeanne was born in Domrémy, Lorraine, our province. She has been a special heroine to the people here these hundreds of years, and to all of France and beyond, the symbol of patriotism. Her birthday became a national holiday, celebrated the second Sunday in May.

Geography lessons gave our teacher scope to stir enthusiasm for the land. We looked at maps showing us the location and features of each region. We saw pictures of the three little flowers that had come to symbolize the tricolor of our flag

– *les bleuets, les marguerites* and *les coquelicots*, growing blue, white and red in northern wheat fields. Our teacher talked about *"la patrie,"* the homeland. She used expressions like *"la grandeur et la gloire."* *"Grandeur"* derived from *"grand"* – big or great. *"Gloire"* wasn't in my vocabulary. The sound of it pleased me though. I was confident it meant something good.

People outside of school seemed ardent about the nation too. I couldn't know this but our province had for years been absorbed into Germany. Only at the end of World War I was it returned to France. The men and women of Lorraine wanted to keep it that way. I sensed the high emotions around me. I liked watching the flags, their three colors bright in the wind. Soldiers marched by singing, *"En passant par la Lorraine avec mes sabots…"* We sang that song at school. I knew every verse.

At home I drew a large heart on a sheet of paper. I filled it with a bouquet of *bleuets, marguerites* and *coquelicots*. This was my first picture not traced or copied or made by coloring between the lines. In it were all my feelings, all I needed to say about me and France. Around this time I composed my own going to sleep prayer. I asked God to protect my parents, my sister and my relatives on the other side of the river. I asked Him to take care of my *"patrie."*

Rarely did I think "France" without that word bringing others along. Words like "beautiful" and "mine."

The only boys I met belonged to friends of my parents. (French elementary schools were for boys or girls, never both in the same building.) When we vacationed in the mountains

26

with another family, Roger, the son, walked by my side, pulled up forget-me-nots and presented them to me. In the city he invited me to his house, where we played with his metal construction set. Henri was also the son of family friends. He was very handsome, adored, spoiled, conceited and not as bright as he believed himself to be. Roger and Henri were nine and I was seven. Both seemed to like me. I had no trouble deciding which of them I preferred.

School progressed happily that first year, setting a pattern. I would always enjoy it. Learning wasn't hard for me. I never questioned my belonging. Being the only Jewish child in the room brought no problems - even though my behavior, one day every week, made this special status impossible to ignore. Each Saturday, classes were held in the morning. It was the Sabbath for me but I went to school anyway, so as not to spoil my attendance record. Having arrived, I could do nothing but look on while the others cut and pasted, sewed, embroidered, painted. This was the day for arts and crafts. I would have loved to join in, but every activity violated the prohibition against work. At last my mother picked me up. She took me and Edith to a café where we ate éclairs.

In June, at year's end, I won prizes - separate ones for the different subjects and one overall, the *Prix d'Excellence*. I didn't quite understand it, except that suddenly I had an armful of new books (books being the prizes). Maman had to cope with them when she arrived with the car. Flabbergasted and thrilled, she drove straight to Papa's office.

Papa said, "You can have anything in the world. What would you like?"

Faced with an endless field of choices I remembered my first and only worldly transaction: the exchange, in Diemeringen, of a bucket of snails for two francs. An enormous sum, I was sure.

"Two francs," I answered.

When the following June brought the same prizes and Papa made the same offer I knew better, being eight instead of seven. I said, "A bicycle." I had it picked out, having seen just such a one go by on the street. I even knew the color. But by then war was looming. Much as he wanted to make good on his promise, Papa had no time for bicycles.

Chapter 6

"Ssh," Maman would say, "Papa is listening to the news."

Papa had always followed the news but starting with the summer before grade two, this became an incessant obsession. Even at mealtime. Breakfast and lunch ceased to be relaxing. The radio in the salon was kept on at all times, and in order to hear it in the adjoining dining room, absolute silence had to be observed. No sooner did Edith or I try to say anything, Maman would sternly remind us, "Papa is listening." Except for the voice on the radio, there was somber silence at the table.

I didn't know why. I was too young to be concerned with the growing unquiet in the world. Any adult would have heard the rumble. Sarreguemines had been a battlefield many times. Papa's ear was super sensitive. He recognized this storm, having fled from it once already, changing countries, uprooting his family.

When I entered second grade I wondered about my classmates. Did their parents read newspapers anxiously? Did no one speak at the dinner table so that the grown-ups could give complete attention to the radio? I visited my friends. Their parents didn't look worried. My teachers said nothing. But whenever adults gathered, the bits of conversation I picked up were usually about events in the world – events that were coming closer, that would soon be difficult to ignore. Maman

and Papa weren't the only ones with this topic on their minds.
And yet my parents were different. For them the threat was
personal, like an arrow pointed at us. Was it because we had
given up our home in Saarbrücken on account of Hitler? My
parents would have known that he had broken the Treaty of
Versailles and was rapidly rearming his country, turning Germany
into a military state. He had expanded the nation's borders and
planned to do so again and again. Our family was at high risk.
Hitler made no secret of his hatred for the Jewish people. How
did my neighbors feel? Were they repelled when Hitler ranted
over the airwaves? Did some of them agree with him?

Fall edged toward winter - September, October, November.
November 9 and 10, 1938. All over Germany synagogues were
set on fire. Jewish books were burned. Shops owned by Jews
were stoned and looted. Jews were attacked in the streets and in
their homes, sometimes by people they knew. These terrible days
and nights would ever after be known as *Kristallnacht* - Night of
Broken Glass.

Before long we learned that our relatives hadn't escaped the
violence. Neighbors of Aunt Berthe and Uncle Nathan had
broken into their home, robbing and destroying. These "new
Nazis" savagely humiliated my aunt in front of her husband
and sons. Many Jews were arrested and imprisoned. My uncles
Nathan and Ernst were sent to Dachau, the first concentration
camp in Germany. Uncle Nathan was released in six weeks
because he already had the papers allowing him and his family
to emigrate from Germany to America. Uncle Ernst never got out.

The letter said he died of pneumonia. Uncle Nathan told us the truth. He had watched guards taunt Ernst, who suffered from a mental illness. When Ernst shouted back the guard beat him without mercy. He was taken to the prison hospital but didn't live long. In the end he might have contracted pneumonia. No one can say. Apparently lots of prisoners died of "pneumonia."

By January, 1939 his children, cousins Lucie and Leon, had come to live with us. Their mother - Papa's sister Gusta - stayed behind to dispose of the family business. Almost as soon as they arrived Leon fell ill with diphtheria. Maman nursed him day and night. Every Friday evening before the Sabbath she helped - nearly carried - him to the living room so he could telephone his mother, who didn't know he was sick and was never told.

In time, our enlarged household found its rhythm. Papa and I and Leon went off to work and school. Maman, assisted by Sophie and niece Lucie, presided over our home. The girls were the same age and got along well. Five year-old Edith followed and watched. She wanted to be exactly like Maman. She dusted and neatly rearranged the toys we shared, creating her own sense of order. We all came together for the main meal at midday, Papa too. Suppers in the evening were simple - farina with milk and sugar and cinnamon, or bread with strawberries and fresh cream. Maman and Papa ate alone later.

I readily accepted the addition of Lucie to our family. I could have done without Leon. At only eleven he pressed his attentions on fifteen year-old Sophie! To me he could be a bully. He enlisted two buddies and the three of them put me in a trash can - empty but smelly - and covered it with a lid. They thought it was a joke.

The cousins had been with us a month when I celebrated my eighth birthday. Friends from school came to the party, as did Roger and the spoiled Henri. During a game of musical chairs they fought over rights to the seat next to mine. Henri, who started the shoving match, came out worse. Afterwards he bore a small scar over his right eyebrow.

In June, we welcomed our grandmother, the formidable Oma. She was eighty-three. Nothing had prepared her for the upheavals she now suffered. Her mind was clear enough but she couldn't accept or absorb all the changes. Forced from her home, her family dispersed, a son-in-law - my Uncle Ernst - dead, she looked about in disbelief. If she were nicer it would have been easier to sympathize.

I pleased her but she wasn't happy with Edith. My sister had somehow failed her by not being born a boy. Oma tolerated any amount of loutish behavior from Leon. He, the namesake of her departed husband, could do no wrong. His crude language and indifferent hygiene went unremarked. When Maman tried to direct him or set limits she interfered. She also objected to what she understood as Maman's inability to tell the difference between family and hired help. Maman, Sophie and Lucie shared the chores. Maman treated both girls warmly. Oma, annoyed to see Lucie working, would say, "Let the maid do it!" Of course Sophie, who was busy also, stood plainly within earshot.

If nerves jangled, I could at least escape to school. And Papa, away at work every day, was preoccupied with business. A devoted son, he wasn't fully aware of how his mother tested his wife's patience. Maman, fearing what stress would do to him, kept it that way. She became the sponge that absorbed tensions.

Our apartment was filled to capacity and straining. Edith and I moved into Maman and Papa's bedroom to make room for Oma and the cousins. I didn't understand how this must have affected my parents' marriage. At the age of eight some things were beyond me. But I was no longer the four year-old who ran free in the meadows while Maman scrubbed, cleaned and cared for a sick baby. I could sense how pressured her life had become. Inwardly I turned toward her. She must have felt it because she drew closer to me. We were becoming friends.

One day we went off in search of a kosher chicken for the Friday night meal. Our home was kosher in general but not in all the particulars - not in the particular of chicken. From Diemeringen days Maman had got in the habit of buying her chicken from the farmers' market along with butter and eggs. Nobody thought about it. Even Papa, more religious than the rest of us didn't seem to care. But Oma had always kept a strict kitchen. She expected no less of us.

Maman and I set out toward the center of town. I had no idea where we were going. After about ten minutes we arrived at a row house. We entered a doorway that led to a courtyard where chickens scampered and squawked. A big man in a white apron reached down. He chose a bird and without further ado stretched its neck on a block and chopped its head off. Then he plucked the feathers from its twitching headless form. Maman and I froze in horror. I don't remember anything more about the man or his house or how we got out of there with our parcel.

Over Papa's desk in the smoking room hung a portrait of his father, Oma's husband, the Opa who died before I was born. He was handsome, with a thick mustache and kind smile. I'd heard how strong he was and wished I could have known him. Periodically my grandmother would stop, stand in front of the picture and talk, sighing and wringing her hands. I could never make out the words. But Maman knew this routine well. Oma had been at it long before moving in with us. She was complaining to the photograph about her daughters-in-law. There were only two so that had to include my mother.

Chapter 7

By the summer of 1939 I couldn't walk outside without seeing tanks. They looked like giant monsters. Sandbags and cannons guarded the streets leading to the courthouse, the Palais de Justice. Barricades surrounded the Palais. Soldiers had always trained in our border town, living in barracks called the Caserne. Now uniformed men were everywhere, their numbers swelling with new recruits. The soldiers tied explosives to the bridge over the Sarre River, in case the Germans tried to cross. Women from the Red Cross stood on the sidewalks, showing anyone who would listen how to use gas masks. There was much talk of these masks and puzzlement over what to do with the hideous things. People were also discussing the "Maginot Line" - a system of miles and miles of trenches and tunnels and all kinds of equipment. They said it was supposed to protect us but they didn't sound persuaded. In my mind the tanks and sandbags were part of the Maginot Line. They weren't. Despite all I heard and saw I wasn't afraid. I was with my family. As long as we were together, nothing that happened then or that war would later bring, was too much for me.

The banks were closed. They had picked up and moved deeper into France. Other government offices did the same. My parents had been worrying for some time about what to do if things got worse. A year ago we'd begun going off on short trips - to a spa, a hotel, a rented room. We'd pile into the car, Maman the driver. She'd start singing once we were on the road, Edith and I joining in. At first Papa would stay quiet. He liked listening to us and was aware he couldn't carry a tune. But eventually a droning sound that corresponded to no known notes began to confuse our melodies. Papa would smile. He knew what he was doing.

Once settled in our vacation spot we would take long walks. The country paths led us over uneven ground. Papa relied on a cane for support. (He rarely used it in the city, where he was chauffeured most of the time.) It was made of polished wood and had a round carved handle and a rubber tip. I couldn't imagine a sight more elegant than my father in his fedora hat and three-piece suit, holding his cane. Maman and Papa hadn't announced the real purpose of these holidays. They were investigating areas further inland, away from the border, in case we suddenly had to leave our home.

On August 23, 1939, Hitler and Stalin signed the Nonaggression Pact. Now Hitler could go forward with his plans to invade Poland knowing Russia wouldn't stop him. (Russia, from the east, intended to invade Poland too. In this way Germany and Russia would divide the smaller country between them.) France and England had sworn to protect Poland. The next morning my father said, "This means war. We must go this very day."

Papa's chauffeur came within hours, bringing the car for Maman to drive. Papa's foreman arrived with a truck for our belongings. When a policeman asked, "Where did you get that truck?" the foreman realized that it might have to be turned over to the government - and soon. The army was on the lookout for every available truck. He told us to hurry. Chaotically we loaded what was ready and were forced to abandon what wasn't.

Other than clothing, some linens and a few dishes, we left most things behind - our fine crystal, silver and china, our artwork and library. We left most of our family photographs - even my favorite picture of Papa, taken after World War I, his head wrapped in bandages revealing a face that looked so like mine. Nearly all our furniture remained, plus Maman's sewing machine which she really needed, and the Persian rugs, stored in mothballs. The large portrait of Opa stayed on the wall. I guess we expected to be back before long.

We split up for the ride. Papa and I were in the car with Maman, along with Oma, Lucie and Edith. Ahead of us in the truck were the foreman (driving), Leon and Sophie. Sophie should have returned to her family but she insisted on staying with us. There was no time to argue.

By late morning we were on the road under a clear August sky. I didn't know where we were going. My parents hadn't told me, probably because they weren't sure either. Maman tried to keep close behind the truck. Then, traffic came between and we lost sight of it. The car broke down. All attempts to revive it failed. We waited by the side of the road until the foreman noticed our disappearance, retraced his route and found us. We piled onto the back of the open truck. Sophie and Leon gave their places in the cab to Papa and Oma and joined us on the flatbed among the trunks and valises. We were off again. The truck hummed along at a steady speed. We started to sing – Edith and I, Lucie, Leon and Sophie - songs like *"Auprès de Ma Blonde"* and *"Au Clair de la Lune"* or rounds of *"Frère Jacques."* Maman came in whenever she knew the words. The combination of fresh air, movement, the sound of our own voices, held us in a kind of trance. We forgot yesterday and tomorrow as we watched the soft green hills of Lorraine roll by. Papa delighted in the fine weather and our singing. It would have been a perfect afternoon, he said, if not for the rest of the circumstances.

When we reached the tiny village of Longeville-en-Barrois the foreman would take us no further. He was to be inducted into the army the next day back in Sarreguemines. Our truck would very likely be inducted too! It was already dusk. We knew no one and nothing in the village we had chanced upon deep in the Lorraine countryside. I don't recall how we spent the night.

Maman was put in touch with a Mme. Chevalier, an elderly widow who had a large house and was willing to have us rent a section of it. The two rooms we were given hadn't been occupied or cleaned for years. A film of dust covered every surface. Fleas infested the beds and upholstery and the place was overrun with mice. Every night traps were set for them. When they were caught they cried like babies. I couldn't bear the sound.

Madame Chevalier was about the same age as Oma. They sat on the front stoop all day complaining to each other. Oma spoke no French and Madame Chevalier no German. They trusted sighs, exclamations and gestures to fill the divide. Each seemed to be getting what she required of the other. Oma would detail her problems in extra-loud German, shaking her head and raising her hands and eyes to heaven. Madame Chevalier would nod sympathetically and offer a rundown of her woes in French - using her hands to get the message across. I think they were trying to share memories and stories from World War I.

School started for Leon, me, and now Edith, six years old and a first grader. Lucie, at sixteen, remained at home. Sophie still refused to leave, although my parents weren't happy about being responsible for her. It couldn't have been the accommodations that made her want to stay. Even forgetting the mice and fleas, there wasn't much space. I shared an alcove with the girls. Leon was on the couch. Oma and my parents slept in the one bedroom.

Edith and I never had many toys, and we had even fewer since our sudden move. But we had succeeded in keeping our two favorite dolls. They were made of celluloid and dressed in outfits knitted by Maman. My sister's *bébé* was the color of chocolate. This was no accident, for Maman wanted us to accept people in all their variety. Edith kissed her doll so often the paint on the nose wore off, leaving it pink.

Winter brought dark mornings and windows covered with the tracings of frost. There was no hot water for bathing so we used the cold. Maman and Sophie plunged their hands into ice water when they did the wash. And it felt more like night than day when Edith, Leon and I started the long walk to school.

We navigated the village streets, our wooden shoes leaving their impressions in the snow. Always there was snow, though we rarely saw it come down. The crystal flakes must have waited until we slept to add a fresh powdery layer to the plain face of Longeville. We trudged past blocks of row houses before reaching the town square with its *mairie*, fountain and church. The boys' school was there. Abandoning Leon, Edith and I continued a short distance beyond the church to our school.

We settled on the outside steps and prepared to work on our feet, numb from the cold. We had lined our *sabots* with newspaper but it was never enough. Frostbite threatened. Like the other children we removed our socks and shoes, dipped our feet in the snow and rubbed them with our hands. We wiggled our toes and felt them tingle as the flow of blood improved. Later, in class, we could warm them by the wood-burning stove. We knew never to put our feet by the fire before they had been rubbed with snow and the circulation restored. To forget and seek warmth too soon would cause terrible pain.

School let out twice a day, first at noon, so we could eat the main meal at home with our families, then finally at four.

By late afternoon there was little light. I soon finished my homework. We didn't get much. Then I'd relax on my bed, my favorite books piled beside me. I had won them the year before in Sarreguemines for the *Prix d'Excellence*. That was when I asked Papa for a bicycle and he promised he'd get it but didn't. I hardly cared now since my wonderful books took me beyond the range of any bicycle. The only problem was what to read first. I had a volume of fairytales by Perrault. Everything in this collection happened long ago and far away, usually in an enchanted forest. I liked to imagine how the characters looked. Their names installed themselves in my memory. *Peau d'Ane* (Donkey Skin), *Le Petit Poucet* (Tom Thumb), *Le Petit Chaperon Rouge* (Little Red Riding Hood), *Le Chat Botté* (Puss 'n' Boots), *Cendrillon* (Cinderella). I suffered with them through their numerous misfortunes and ordeals, but knew I could count on the stories to end happily. I had books about modern children too. Not really modern, but closer to me in time than the magical inhabitants of fairy tales. *Les Petites Filles Modèles* followed the doings of well-brought-up nineteenth century girls. They were my age and almost perfect. I wasn't convinced by them or their very tame escapades. I preferred another book – *Les Malheurs de Sophie* – about a girl who couldn't do anything right, whose every step was a misstep. She bumbled her way through life, in trouble no matter what. I spent many contented afternoons in her amusing company.

Before supper, Maman, Edith and I might stop and wonder at the brief, blazing sunset. Looking out, only Oma could find fault with the sky. Such violence of color, she observed, was a sure omen of bloody battles to come. Maman was aware of the superstition. She didn't wish to share it with her daughters. To plant fears made no sense to her. And she wouldn't have wanted to deprive us of joy in Longeville's moment of genuine beauty.

France had been officially at war since September. As schoolchildren we were incorporated into the patriotic effort. We wanted to believe we made a difference. Our third grade class felt sorry for the young soldiers from the African colonies who were being sent to fight in freezing northern Europe. From our geography lessons we knew they had never seen snow or ice, and this was a particularly bitter winter. We "adopted" a soldier from Madagascar. We had his picture. His name was Gabriel and his skin was dark like that of Edith's doll. We sent him sugar cubes, cakes, chocolate bars, dried fruit and preserves, all brought from home, scarce foods we would have otherwise eaten. Several afternoons a week we knitted for him - scarves, mittens, sweaters, socks, gloves. While we worked one student read aloud from the Greek myths. I was fascinated by the gods, muses and nymphs. In the next room the first graders were knitting too. Since they were beginners, they stuck to scarves.

I was conscious of being the one Jewish girl in my class. I had managed that way in Sarreguemines without problems and didn't expect them here. By early winter I discovered I wasn't going to be alone in the minority. A Gypsy caravan stopped in Longeville and a girl just older than I joined our class. She was with us for a few months. By early spring the caravan would move on. That's how her life was – not staying long enough in any school to learn basic skills. She couldn't participate in classwork so the rest of us thought she was dull. It didn't help that she had lice in her long thick blue-black hair. We all avoided her.

The presence of the Gypsy girl didn't make me less unusual. Gypsies passed through the village every year. My classmates had never seen a Jew.

Early in 1940, Germany was advancing through Belgium and the skies overhead buzzed with action. Planes were fighting in the air. Sometimes there was flying debris. Sirens went off during the school day and we were taken from the building to wait out danger in the wine cellar of a nearby house. The teachers sent one or two gas masks around the room. We took turns holding them, turning them this way and that while the teachers demonstrated their use. Nobody really understood how they worked. They didn't even fit faces of varying sizes. By the time any of us could have figured out how to wear one it wouldn't have mattered. Later, the teachers led the classes in the *Pater noster* and *Ave Maria*. I listened to the prayers. I hoped no one noticed I wasn't saying them.

What I wanted most that year was to join the Girl Scouts. In Longeville that meant *Les Guides*, a Catholic organization. Some of my classmates already belonged to it. I went with them. We met Sunday mornings at the parish house or the *mairie*. Our leader was a young woman from one of the large, land-owning families. When weather permitted - it was early spring - we hiked up the hills into the beautiful vineyard country. We wore little boots that ended above our ankles to protect us from snakes. Vipers crawled in the grass and hid under loose, slate-like stones. Our leader said, "If anyone is bitten by a snake cut across the puncture with a pocketknife, suck the venom into your mouth and spit it out." I listened, pocketknife in hand, proud to be acquiring these crucial skills. Luckily, I didn't have to practice what I learned. We climbed the hills singing. At the top we visited people in a farmhouse, exchanged greetings, drank water from their pump and rested awhile. Marching down we sang again. There was a small river at the bottom of the hill. We'd sit and watch the frogs and tadpoles and harmless water snakes that populated it. In the quieter pools swam blood-sucking leeches - ugly, frightening, fascinating.

On rainy Sundays we went to the church for mass. I knelt with the others but when they prayed I kept an uneasy silence. After this happened several times, the group leader called me aside. My behavior at mass had been observed. It would be best, she said, if I didn't continue with Les Guides. Her words stung. I had never before been singled out because I wasn't Christian. Afterwards I hated not going on the hiking trips and I missed the girls. I saw them at school. Most treated me exactly the same and we were still friends. One wanted to inspect my scalp. She pushed aside my hair expecting to find horns. This had something to do with my being Jewish, though I didn't know what. She wasn't mean about it, just curious, as if asking for a better look at someone's freckles.

That spring we moved to a rented house on the outskirts of town. Suddenly we had rooms enough inside and land all around. A local carpenter made us a few pieces of furniture. Life was nearly normal. Sophie said goodbye at last and returned to her family. She had been with us for years and seemed almost like a sister. It was strange at first looking at the accustomed places and not finding her. Then, something new focused my thoughts and energy. The carpenter's cat had a litter and Maman let me adopt a tiny gray tiger-striped kitten. He was my first pet. I called him Micki. Soon after, a cat from the fields set up housekeeping in our attic. She was expecting a litter. The kittens were born in March or April. The mother cat went out for long periods hunting, so Maman, Edith and I assisted her by feeding the infants with our doll baby bottles. I didn't catch colds often, but when I did I loved staying home with Micki and our independent mother cat and a basket of kittens. I could continue to knit for Gabriel on my own. If I got stuck Oma was happy to help me.

Soon it was warm enough to work in the garden. I had my own section. I found a big stock pot, dug a hole and put it in the ground. I dipped a bucket in the little brook that flowed by the back fence of our land and poured the clear water into the sunken pot. Rain added to it. In time the pot became a pond. Flowers grew around it. I transplanted a young pine tree so there would be shade. Finally I went to the river that ran through Longeville, captured a small green frog and placed him at the edge of the pond. He stayed! Soon other frogs and tadpoles and little inedible snails joined him. Our whole family took part in planting the rest of the garden. We grew berry bushes, strawberry patches and rows of radishes, cucumbers, peas and green beans.

The war was moving toward us. After the cats arrived, so did some French officers. They decided that several rooms in our house would make excellent offices. They didn't sleep over but spent every day with us. They were very polite. They respected Papa as soldiers honor another who has paid the price defending his country. It didn't matter to them that he had been on the other side. He'd had no choice about being called up to serve. The soldiers in our house ate Maman's best coffee cakes and butter cookies, and flirted with her. When we took our walks in the vineyard, each vied to be the one who offered her his arm.

At school we tried to keep our minds on arithmetic, on the stories we were learning, on poems we recited by heart and copied into our *cahiers*, our notebooks. Our lessons were constantly interrupted. We could never predict when the wail of sirens and the roar of dogfighting planes would send us hurrying out of the building into the wine cellar of the neighboring house. If air raids caught us in the fields, far from shelter, we were instructed to immediately stretch out on the grass.

It must have been hard for Edith, starting first grade under these conditions. She had delicate features and pale blonde hair and was as fragile as she looked. Held close to home during her early years, she was unused to the rough, careless play of children and the sharp voices of strange adults. She'd heard mostly German from our family and had no French friends. Now she had to learn a new language all at once. Her teacher offered no extra attention or special kindness. From the beginning, Edith would have to struggle in ways I was spared.

46

Yet, as I drew strength from my parents, so did she. She trusted me, too, following eagerly whenever I wanted to include her, waiting to hear my adventures when she couldn't come along. If dodging the effects of warplanes was part of a curriculum that I accepted, she was prepared to do the same. She ran home from school one afternoon poised to share the very latest safety tip. She was sure she had it right. "Listen, everybody! If a bomb hits you, lie down flat!"

Chapter 8

The bomb that hit us didn't fall from the sky. It was less a bomb than a boulder, rolling from atop a high hill, pausing, then picking up speed and force for the final descent. It took a while to flatten us.

The first signs of trouble came early in the spring of 1940. Authorities in Longeville told Papa he had better go to Bar-le-Duc - the major city nearby - to straighten out his papers. Papa made the trip accompanied by a lawyer, Maman and three friends who lived in Bar-le-Duc and could vouch for his character. The interview went smoothly and the officials looked satisfied. They requested only that he appear at the military barracks before leaving. Papa complied. Papers in hand, he presented himself to the officers and answered questions. Go home to Longeville, they directed him, and come back with a metal plate and cutlery. Startled, he asked, "Am I to be detained here?"

They said, "Yes."

Papa returned to Longeville supposedly to get his supplies. Instead he paid an urgent call on the town commandant. He demanded to see an army doctor, the one person who could provide proof that he was not a threat to the French nation. A doctor was summoned and soon Papa got the medical statement he needed. Back in Bar-le-Duc, the officers seemed to accept the doctor's verdict. Papa thought this would be the end of it.

Some weeks passed - a month or more? It was ten o'clock at night in early May. We were in bed except for Papa, who heard the knocking. He opened the door to find himself staring at the point of a fixed bayonet.

A stony-faced officer was holding the weapon. He escorted Papa from the house. Maybe other soldiers were there, though I didn't know for sure. They rode in a truck to a building where Papa was questioned. What had he done as a soldier in World War I? How long had he been in France? Why had he come? Papa produced the medical certificate confirming his injuries and disabilities. The officer looked at it and at Papa. "I see our French shrapnel worked well," he said, his lip curling in a sneer. Papa was shocked. Soldiers, like the ones who had stayed with us, usually showed immediate sympathy for a wounded veteran, no matter who he was or on which side he had fought.

The bayonet man told Papa that he and Maman could expect to be taken into custody soon. Having heard this, my father was allowed to leave. Nothing was said about the rest of the family.

A week later, I was in school on a warm Friday afternoon. I remember the date - May 17, 1940. Sirens sounded. We hurried from our classes, outdoors and down to the familiar wine cellar. It was dark as we sat on the floor. There was only one small window. It was probably covered. When the two policemen - the *gendarmes* – arrived, they called for us by name: Renée and Edith Kann. My sister and I followed them up the uneven steps of earth and wood, squinting in the sun when we reached the top. The *gendarmes* walked us home. They gave Maman one hour to pack for the seven of us.

Papa and Oma were taken first. They were allowed the comforts of an automobile. An open truck awaited my mother, Edith and me, Leon and Lucie.

Once again we were riding, jostling through the French countryside to an unknown place. This time there was no singing, no enthusiasm for scenery. Our circumstances, not good on the previous trip, were, needless to say, worse now. We sat squeezed uncomfortably among our suitcases. From their size and number I concluded that we weren't coming back soon. Who would take care of my cat, Micki? And the kittens in the attic - who would feed them while their *maman* went hunting in the fields?

Our destination was a jail in Bar-le-Duc. We were housed with other women and children. Each family group huddled together, showing no interest in anyone else. The words I could hear, the whispers and murmurs, were of many languages and accents. Our cell had been a horse stable - until very recently, to judge from the smell. It was airless and hot, with straw mats on an earth floor. On the other side of the stable-cell were latrines. Odors from that room seeped into ours and droplets of moisture collected on our side of the common wall. Little daylight penetrated the clouded windows above the door. We didn't know what was happening to Oma and Papa. Later, Papa told us.

He and my grandmother were put in a room in the main building. Papa did his best to hide the fact that they were captives. Oma regarded with suspicion the locks on the doors and the multitude of keys people wielded. She needed to use the washroom and told a policeman. He disappeared, then returned with a bucket which he stationed in the middle of the room. He withdrew and secured the door. "Are we in jail?" my grandmother asked. Papa couldn't deny it. She broke into tears. Oma came to us late the same afternoon, distraught and unsteady.

Maman was frantic with worry about Papa. She feared that without special care he would become ill. Marshalling strength and all her charm, she approached the guards. She explained Papa's condition and, persuaded, they took her to him. From then on she was allowed regular visits.

On the third day they came and removed our belongings. A prison matron searched us, including Edith and me. She made us stand while her hands explored our bodies head to toe, back and front, up between our legs. We were seven and nine. She undid the curl on Edith's head that Maman had carefully pinned. What could it possibly conceal? Was the policewoman, like my classmate from Les Guides, looking for horns?

In fact, none of this was happening to us because we were Jews. It was happening because we had been born on the German side of a river, and because Papa had fought for Germany in World War I. Being foreign was what we had in common with everyone in our cell. France was at war and afraid of foreigners, especially foreigners from Germany. Being Jewish should have counted in our favor. As targets of Hitler's greatest hatred, we were unlikely to spy for him. Nobody seemed to think of that.

We weren't treated with particular cruelty. The guards brought food three times a day. It wasn't bad. When darkness fell the rats came out. It was impossible to lie down because they darted across our faces. But Edith and I could sit on our straw mats, lean against Maman, stare across at the gray silent figures in the shadows, or up at the dim glow of the lightbulbs. We breathed the stale air and tried to keep clear of the damp, foul-smelling wall. And when it was very late or very early, we slept.

Chapter 9

First there were trucks, then a train. The whole jail at Bar-le-Duc seemed to have emptied onto the train. I recognized our cellmates from the stable. There were others I hadn't seen before. At least Papa was with us now. Like everyone on board except the soldiers, we had been taken from jail but not released. An onlooker, seeing our train, wanting to know who we were, just had to read the large letters painted on the side of the cars: *Prisonniers de guerre* – prisoners of war.

The seven of us rode in an enclosed section. Two wooden benches faced each other, and above us hung net hammocks for our belongings. We only had light hand luggage. The trunks, they said, were going separately on freight cars. Warm dusty air blew in through the open windows, making us cough. Smells and grit of the train, track and coal-fired engine mingled with the sweat of people confined too long in narrow compartments in the heat of summer. Outside an untroubled landscape passed before our eyes. Golden wheat fields sprinkled with tiny blue flowers – *les bleuets*. And red poppies – *les coquelicots*.

When the train stopped to be resupplied with water we were allowed to get off and fill our cups at the faucets. This must not have happened many times because I remember being thirsty. I don't remember being hungry even though there was never enough to eat. What food there was the soldiers were giving to a group of young women. So we all believed.

The women wore contented, well-fed expressions. During stopovers we tried to buy chocolate but the vendors wouldn't sell to us. One refused to lend Papa a can opener, telling him he might as well eat the metal. We were the enemy, branded by the sign on the train.

We had to take turns in order to sleep. Leon found a place on the floor. The adults dozed sitting up. Lucie laid her head on Oma's lap and I rested mine on Maman's. Edith fit into the overhead hammock and nestled against our parcels. When Papa needed a whole bench for himself, the displaced ones would walk for a while.

We'd been riding three days. I was more curious than uncomfortable. Edith, Leon and Lucie were holding up too, though the lack of food was hard on Leon. We got one loaf of bread each evening to be divided among seven people. It had to last twenty-four hours since nothing else would be offered. Leon watched Maman slice the bread. He finished his portion and begged her to give him an "advance" on breakfast. "Please, please, please," he repeated. He was in a growth spurt and needed more to eat but Maman refused to give in. His eyes desperate, he would have lunged forward and taken it. Papa held him. The next morning he was grateful my parents had stood firm.

Mostly though, we children were doing better than the adults. Our experience, strange and unsettling as it was, seemed to us an adventure. The grown-ups, weary and increasingly convinced that nothing made sense, struggled to keep brave faces. Suddenly Oma wanted her favorite hat. Where was it? Had Maman remembered to bring it? Yes? Then find it! Maman eased a bundle down from the netting and began to pull everything apart. She was searching for a black straw hat decorated with shiny black and white cherries. At last it was discovered, but in disappointing condition, the stiff material somewhat squashed. Oma was outraged. Why hadn't Maman packed it better? The full sum of my grandmother's anger, fear and frustration fixed on the insult to her precious hat. Oma continued to berate Maman who was upset anyway and in no state to accept a rant. The train was moving quickly. Papa, who never interfered, who was the most devoted of sons, grabbed the hat from his mother's hands and threw it out the window. It went sailing like a disk over yellow swaying wheat into the blue sky. Papa was quite athletic with his good arm. We were speechless, even Oma.

As the train progressed we left the north behind and entered the Rhône Valley. Fields of grain gave way to vineyards. We stopped at the town of St. Etienne and spent the night at an old monastery. We ate good food and slept on cots. In the morning we boarded a second train that was continuing south, but slowly. We crammed into quarters so small no one could sleep. The bread and water they gave us didn't begin to ward off hunger and thirst. Still, I was eager with anticipation, my mind held by the prospect of one thing. Sooner or later we would reach the Mediterranean Sea.

The train threaded its halting path. Often we had to wait,

delayed at one station or another. But in time I noticed the light changing, the colors more intense. I saw dark, low cypress trees and flowering acacias, their blossoms white against a brilliant sky. Then, through the trees, I glimpsed a stripe of turquoise – the calm, clear *Méditerranée*. I'd read about it, imagined it, always dreamed I'd travel to it, though not like this. My attention rarely wavered from the window. I didn't want to miss the unpredictable, fleeting appearances of water and sand. I tried to spot every sliver of blue and patch of pale beach until the train shifted direction and the sea vanished for good.

We were heading west. The train, having made an L-turn away from the shoreline, was moving into the wooded hills of the interior.

We stumbled off at a nameless town and were loaded immediately onto trucks. Papa couldn't balance. He lay on the floor. Exhausted, we were beyond caring exactly where we were. With the sea behind me and nothing definite to draw me forward I felt my spirits sag. We had the clothes we were wearing and the few supplies we were carrying, but where were the trunks, the ones supposedly being shipped by freight?

It had been eight days since we were taken from the jail at Bar-le-Duc. Less than two hours into our truck ride we could look out and realize the journey was over. Below, over a vast flat land spread rows of wooden barracks fenced with barbed wire. A metallic coating covered the roofs and made the light glare back into our eyes. Despite the sunny weather there was something dismal and forbidding about this place, our destination. And institutional. A sort of badly chosen holiday camp, I thought. In the distance snow-capped mountains cut the sky like great jagged teeth. I knew the mountains were called the Pyrenees. On the other side was Spain.

Chapter 10

Without warning Maman grasped our hands and veered sharply to the side. Edith and I nearly lost our footing. But it was too late. We had already seen the man in the wheelbarrow. It was being pushed by his companions who stopped now and then to check on his comfort. He had no arms and no legs.

We were stunned, though we didn't speak of it that day or ever. Maman had once wanted to be a nurse and wasn't afraid to look straight at the calamities that can befall a human life. But the color had gone out of her face. She quickened her step and said, "Hurry, Papa is waiting."

We had arrived two weeks ago. From the moment we entered the barrack we knew Papa wouldn't be able to survive where there were no windows, no furniture, only straw mats on the floor. Getting up and down was impossible for him. Doorways at either end of the long room let in a little light and air. Something like tin foil was fixed to the roof in order to deflect the sun's strong rays. Enough got through. Inside and out the heat was unrelenting. Our building and the others nearby were just for women and children. My father and cousin Leon were in the men's barracks, where conditions might be harder still. When word came that Papa had been transferred to the infirmary, we were relieved. Maman, Edith and I were making our first visit to see him. We had trekked from our part of the camp over what seemed miles of flat bare terrain the color of ocher.

He lay on a cot in a room with windows. There were other patients on cots and doctors circulating among them. Papa was very weak. He would take time to recover from the days and nights on the train, the heat, the lack of food, the uncertainty. When he saw us his eyes came alive and Maman rushed to him. Even in Bar-le-Duc she hadn't been kept from his side more than twenty-four hours. They clung to each other. Edith and I waited, a bit shyly, for them to make room for us. Papa searched our faces – yes, we were real and well. He said, "Take care of Maman."

Our parents talked and then were quiet, holding hands. Edith and I decided to explore the infirmary. We saw men with every combination of disability. Some were missing arms or legs. Some were blind. No one shocked us like the man in the wheelbarrow. I heard a doctor tell Maman that the hospital housed patients who were – it's hard to believe – worse off. He offered to show her the ward. Before her marriage my mother had worked with children who couldn't walk, children with all kinds of bone problems. She intended to devote her life to them but then she met my father. Maybe Papa had told the doctors this story. That could explain why she was expected to be interested in medical matters. More likely the reason was to be found in Maman herself. There was something compassionate about her, graceful and soothing. She made people feel better when they were near her. Now my father's doctor wanted her to follow him into the room where the worst cases were kept. I heard her thank him but noticed she didn't go.

I looked forward to our visits with Papa and didn't at all mind being inside a hospital. To me it wasn't bleak or depressing. A feeling I couldn't name united the residents. They spoke many languages, must have come from many lands, but it was as if they were all citizens of an imaginary country where helping one another was a primary commandment. I thought about the barrack I shared with Edith and Maman, Oma and Lucie and a collection of strangers. We came from different places and spoke a number of languages too. We had a problem in common. The French government suspected us, considered us "enemy aliens." We got along but anyone wagering he'd find a special understanding or affection among us would have been disappointed. What was it that connected the men of the infirmary?

They were even more impressed with Edith and me than we were with them. They watched us in a state of mind resembling wonder. We might have been day-trippers from a distant star.

I learned there had been a war in Spain. Many of the men were Spanish. The others, the ones speaking Czech, Hungarian, Polish, Russian, had left their own countries to join the International Brigade, enlisting in a desperate struggle to save Spain from fascist dictatorship. They lost.

Making their way over the mountains, those who could walk carried those who couldn't. What would France do with them? The answer was this camp called Gurs, built for the defeated ragtag soldiers of the Spanish Civil War. The hospital where Papa lay was designed for the war injured. The physicians who looked after him had been foreign volunteers, treating the wounded in the field. Everyone we met in the infirmary – doctor and patient – was a veteran of the failed project on the other side of the Pyrenees. Beyond the hospital gates, the camp had until now been made up solely of able-bodied ex-soldiers, most of them Spanish.

Enemies of the victors, none could go back. Nor were they to be permitted freedom in France. Highly political foreigners who had recently taken up arms could hope for a cautious welcome at best. Here at Gurs the authorities were keeping a wary eye on these dreamers, communists, socialists, radicals, uncompromising believers in causes.

Barred from the larger society, the men had become accustomed to a world without children. That was why the simple presence of Edith and me brought them such joy. It was like having an instrument on which certain notes had gone silent and at last no thought is given to hearing them again. Then suddenly, unexpectedly, they are sounded.

My sister and I were observed with concern because of our thinness. In the regular barrack we had little to eat. The infirmary operated under different rules. Those who prepared the food were allowed into town to do the shopping. They added to their lists special items that the patients wanted (and paid for). There was a Spanish captain. He had been wounded but was now strong and able to help his comrades. He enjoyed frequent access to treats. Maybe he had friends in the kitchen. One day he wanted to share something. When he realized we didn't understand his language he knocked two eggs together, proving they were hard-cooked, and gestured that they were for us. He taught us to say, *"Tengo hambre."* I am hungry. We never would have pestered people with this phrase. We didn't need to. Someone always seemed eager to fatten us with chocolates or even a jar of preserves to take back. A Polish pediatrician, aware of our poor diets, pressed vitamins into Maman's hand. The care we got counted. Every child in our barrack suffered from dysentery except for Edith and me.

I was too young to know the words "Spanish Civil War" or "International Brigade." I didn't ask why men would leave their homes when they didn't have to and fight in another people's war. Nobody told me that great nations and small had watched the forces playing out in Spain for indications of what was to come. (What was to come had already started – World War II.) One thing was clear. Maman and Papa admired these patients and doctors, and in conversation seemed almost to revere them. Had we followed the majority religion, my parents could have been talking about the saints.

Anyone could see that the men cared about each other. You could tell, especially once a week when the newspaper arrived. The cook brought it back from town with the groceries. This local paper was always out of date, the information in it probably not reliable even when current. No one minded. The men weren't choosy about their only connection to the outside world.

One person would read aloud in French, converting the important parts into Hungarian, Czech, Russian and Polish. This chosen reader was one of the surprising number of readers fluent in many languages. His audience hung onto every word. When he finished with the paper it was passed to the Spaniards, who took care of their own. Of all the patients in the hospital, they had the highest number of seriously wounded. The war had been theirs, fought on their soil.

After the readings there might have been some discussion. The whole activity lasted no longer than thirty minutes. I've forgotten the faces but not the voices, low and pleasant.

I was on my way to see Papa and had nearly arrived when sounds of singing and clapping stopped me. They were coming from in front of the infirmary, where people had gathered. There were men from the nearby barracks, hospital staff and a few of the stronger patients. A talent show was in progress. Musicians strummed guitars and clicked castanets. Dancers held themselves very straight, heads high, their faces at once haughty and ecstatic. They clapped their hands and stamped their feet against wooden boards set down for them as a stage. Hands and feet together produced impossibly complicated syncopations. Members of the audience called out encouragement and joined in the clapping. Singers stood around the dancers. Their voices, sometimes rough as sandpaper, sometimes rich and liquid, poured out long, haunting, undulating notes or startled us with quick staccato phrases. I was transfixed. I thought of Papa and me in synagogue listening to the cantor. The flamenco I was hearing now and the Hebrew chanting I remembered had far places and the past echoing through them.

Afterwards the performers took their instruments and faded into the landscape. They were Spanish men who lived in the same *îlot* (island) of the camp as the hospital – inmates like all of us. Maybe some had been professionals earlier in their lives. To me they couldn't have been better. I kept hoping they would repeat their magic on another day but they never did. If I saw them, if they walked by as their ordinary selves, I wouldn't have known.

More barracks than needed had been built in Gurs. (Not everyone had fled to France. Many Spaniards had found refuge in Mexico.) There was room for us, the detainees of a new war. Our *îlot* was a long walk from the men's section and the hospital. I lived in a barrack with Maman and Edith, my cousin Lucie and Oma and others unlucky to be caught in the net of suspicion. Maybe there were real spies among us. It was impossible to say. Here we weren't offered chocolates or entertainment or favorite foods purchased in town. Nobody read a newspaper. There was little to distract us from the monotonous landscape and the slow pace of time.

We had bread and water each morning, which at least looked like what it was. Later we had thin soups with hard, flavorless spheres floating in them. We had stews featuring stringy pieces of "mystery" meat. I learned the puzzling little balls were undercooked chickpeas. The source of the meat was never identified. Oma had serious doubts about our definitely not kosher food. But hunger prevailed and she ate.

Maman had been elected "captain." She collected the food and saw that everyone got a fair share. Lucie was her assistant. She was too old to fit in with the children and not old enough to be accepted by the young women. Maman had other tasks like taking headcounts and listening to troubles – the last no less important for being unofficial. At night we lay on the floor. Our beds were cotton sacks filled with straw. The sacks had large floral patterns printed on them. Rats the size of kittens darted in the shadows. My mother, never a deep sleeper, would try to scare them away.

All day long, the sun beat on the wooden walls, causing temperatures indoors to rise. Edith and I wore the dresses we were wearing when we came to Gurs, mine a knitted dress Maman had made for me, and Edith a cotton dress. We also each had a hand-knitted, short-sleeved cardigan. These clothes didn't suit the weather, but we had nothing to change into. The trunks never did arrive. At night we slept in underpants. Each morning we slipped on our dresses and gave Maman the panties to wash. They dried fast in the baking heat. We managed smoothly with this system until early one day a woman, impressed with our handmade outfits, decided to examine Maman's workmanship. She lifted the hem of my skirt. I nearly died of embarrassment.

We'd been at Gurs a week or two when Edith and I found a use for the inedible chickpeas. Removed from the soup and dried in the sun, they made very satisfactory marbles. We spent hours hunched over or sprawled on our knees, shooting small, hard, ocher spheres across flat, hard, ocher earth.

The way was always clear. No grass, no vegetation existed to disrupt the momentum of these tough little rolling balls. We dug a shallow circle - that was the "goal" - and decided how wide the path to it should be. We carved long lines to mark the boundaries of the path and distinguish foul shots from successes. Our game attracted more children and encouraged a fresh attitude toward chickpeas.

We played with the other children. They were with us and around us but I remember only one name: Roland. It belonged to a small boy who attached himself to my sister and me. He appeared one morning at breakfast, seeing that we were applying jam to our bread. He held out his slice, waited while we spread jam on it, ran to his mother, then, back to us. He presented the same piece, licked clean. We obliged him. He repeated this several times, which Edith and I found amusing. We walked with him, kept him company. He was our pet. His mother must have been glad. She was nervous like many mothers of babies and preschoolers. It was hard for women like her who had no adult relatives to help them. Roland's mother didn't even know where her husband had been taken. The little boy gravitated into our child-orbit. Without words he made us understand exactly what he wanted. He was almost three years old, but couldn't or wouldn't talk.

There was a mother who walked calmly with her infant. I loved seeing them go by. She was nineteen or twenty, with long dark hair, olive skin, an oval face. Her walk was like dance. A woman Oma's age accompanied her, her grandmother. Together they tended the baby, rocking it and singing lullabies in a language unknown to me. Oma warmed to the older lady – Oma, who complained about everything, who could barely touch the food, who feared (aloud and constantly) for Papa and Leon. We assured her Papa had good care and Leon – Papa knew this – held his own among the men. Oma worried anyway but at least was finding comfort with the other grandmother. Once again, lack of a common language was no barrier. Sitting side by side, they would share confidences and appeared to understand each other. They would take in the arid expanses and the life around the barracks – mothers and children trying to get through their day, young women smiling and flirting with the tanned slender Spaniards who came from the men's section to fix things, fashion benches from a few boards, empty the latrines.

The dark-haired woman, her baby and her grandmother were Gypsies. It didn't take long for everyone to realize it and shun them. They occupied the worst spot in our barrack – up front, next to the opening, closing door. They knew that no room would be made for them elsewhere. Oma's interest in the grandmother ended abruptly.

Maman and Papa weren't completely free of prejudice. Back in Sarreguemines, when caravans rolled into town for the annual fair and the Gypsies set up camp with their animals and large families, my parents would caution me to keep my distance. But here in Gurs, Maman quickly learned to see with her own eyes. She could never tolerate injustice, and staunchly defended the Gypsy family against false rumors and accusations. When an item vanished and opinion immediately settled on who were the likely thieves, she worked to quash the whispering campaigns. Without exception, the object, misplaced by the owner, surfaced after several days. We had many temporary "losings" but nothing was ever stolen.

The old Gypsy woman told fortunes. She wasn't alone. Fortune-telling was a popular pastime for people with nothing to do, whose lives hung suspended. For those requiring guidance, there was no shortage of seers employing a bewildering variety of methods. Reading palms, reading cards, studying the bumps on a person's skull – these and more were avenues to the desired hidden knowledge. I wasn't sure it was nonsense but I wasn't attracted to it either. Oma was sure. She said it was appalling superstition and not for people like us. She discouraged Lucie from patronizing any of the self-proclaimed soothsayers. My cousin wouldn't have let that stop her if she really wanted her fortune revealed, which she didn't.

Maman tried it. On our visits to Papa she liked to repeat what she had been told – that she was destined to encounter a tall dark stranger. (Papa had reddish blonde hair and a light complexion.) Since the Spanish men were everywhere how could the prediction fail? I was with her on one consultation. An "expert" solemnly felt the topography of her head, checking the normal bumps and angles for clues about the fate of our lost luggage. I didn't see how the one connected with the other.

Sayings and rhymes floated in the air. They linked human and natural events, random things that wouldn't seem to matter.

Araignée le matin – chagrin.
Araignée le soir – espoir.
A spider in the morning – sorrow.
A spider in the evening – hope.

I never again could look at a beautiful dew-studded spiderweb without hoping that I would not also see its inhabitant.

Most of the sayings were warnings. I learned that a bird who makes the mistake of singing in the morning will weep by evening. But some proverbs were sunnier. A ladybug was always lucky. She was a *bête à bon Dieu*, a creature of the good Lord. These phrases, once heard, had a way of sticking. Their reasoning escaped me, but I respected what adults said and paid attention. Oma believed a too red sunset signaled clashing armies. If she could think that, why did she despise fortune-telling? To be on the safe side, if I caught myself singing in the morning I made sure to stop.

Sometimes the sky dulled to an ominous yellow-gray and we hurried for cover. When rain came it was sudden and fierce. The barren land couldn't hold moisture. Water had no place to go. The ground turned slippery and treacherous. To get to the latrines you had to leave the barrack and trudge to another building – a challenge for anyone and frightening and dangerous for the elderly. Otherwise you stayed in. Except for a game of cat's cradle there was nothing to do.

At last clouds broke. The pools and rivulets evaporated into air as hot as if there had been no storm. What was left was mud – mud everywhere. I took some in my hands and shaped new marbles, nice big ones. I set them to dry in the sun. They joined my chickpeas and the mud marbles of previous rains – all fossilized into a condition of near permanence.

Each day I saw flat, yellow brown earth, hot blue sky, and the mountains that drew my eyes like magnets. No matter where I was they were there, mysterious and silver-tipped around the rim of the world. They weren't old, gentle, rounded mountains, but sprung up in dramatic peaks. Never had I been close to anything so high.

One morning nuns from a local convent arrived. They had come to take the children on an excursion into the Pyrenees.

We got on a truck while the mothers and grandmothers looked on anxiously. They'd heard about children being "rescued" who promptly vanished from their parents' lives forever. We had no such cares but rode away happily. The driver steered us up, up, through narrow roads that fell away steeply, past thick forests, to the meadows above the tree line. The truck stopped and the nuns led us further up the hillside. We breathed clean air and the forgotten scent of grass. The colors of the grass and wildflowers, the sounds of birds and insects, the cool breeze on our faces left us astonished and silent. We climbed high enough to see far below, tiny and distant, the barbed wire, the rows of barracks. Gurs. The sight was unbearable. Until then I'd imagined I lived at a not very good summer camp. Looking down, I saw a prison.

We returned to our mothers, proving that we hadn't been kidnapped. They fell on us in relief.

During the days that followed I gazed at the horizon. The mountains had a different meaning now. They beckoned like everything I couldn't reach.

Chapter 11

We got out gradually, not quite realizing it was happening. About a month into our stay, France fell to the Germans, caving in suddenly and completely. That was in June 1940. The news was slow to reach us. We noticed rules becoming lax, the organization of the camp less efficient. It seemed we could visit Papa whenever we wanted.

At last an announcement came that things had changed at the top. The gates were unlocked. They told us transportation was available for anyone wanting to go to Germany, which now included previously French Alsace and Lorraine. Our old apartment was there but we weren't going. Escaping Germany had been our project from the start. We weren't going to let imprisonment at Gurs change our minds. Any awful surprises that might yet lurk in our adopted country couldn't compare to what would await us within the borders of Germany itself. Of that we were sure. The people who chose to go back didn't necessarily admire Hitler. Some probably did. Many just wanted to return to houses and relatives and to what they regarded as an orderly country with promising advantages. (None who held this view were Jewish.) Then there were the ex-soldiers from the Spanish Civil War. Many of them were communists, certain to be executed as soon as the German troops marched in. The French guards spirited the men out of camp in the dark of night.

Most Gurs inmates didn't opt for a return to Germany.

Dozens grabbed their belongings and rushed onto the highways the moment the gates opened. No one knew what was going on or had any way of finding out. There was no communication of news. Restaurants and stores were open but they had little to sell. The local people were staying home, waiting in confusion for whatever occurs after defeat. They were afraid of the refugees who were everywhere, fleeing south and west, putting maximum distance between themselves and the Germans. And the liberated of Gurs, with no idea of what to do, how even to find food, drifted back to the camp. From then on, plans were made more carefully. The barracks emptied piecemeal.

My parents knew they would have to think before we acted. Maman collected five "mattress covers" from bedding abandoned by other families. She sewed them into five knapsacks. Papa bought a wooden valise from the cook. Maman already had two so that made three. At least when we were ready to leave there would be some conveyance for our not very much. We were spending more and more time with Papa until we decided going back and forth was a nuisance. Maman, Edith, Oma, Lucie and I moved into the infirmary. No one cared. There was plenty of room.

Because we were in the south and the heat was intense, Papa could do little but lie on his cot. To improve his strength and allow him better use of his crooked, locked-in-position arm, the doctors had devised special exercises. They worked his arm with weights, pulling and stretching it toward straightness. They gave him baths and massages. We saw progress, though the gains were small and fated to evaporate after the regimen stopped. The attention and devotion of the doctors fortified my father's powerful inner resolve. Despite present weakness – temporary, due only to the heat, he told himself – he was mentally back at the helm of his beloved family, hatching strategies for our next step. We would get away from the hot sun, go north but not too far. We would avoid the Germans, who were occupying the upper half of France.

Leon joined us. Having "graduated" at age twelve from the men's section of Gurs, he was cockier than ever.

Papa's ideas took shape. He telegraphed his brother Nathan in America. The message came back. Yes, of course, Oma and the children, Lucie and Leon, should come to a city called Pittsburgh, in the state of Pennsylvania across the sea. They already had the documents they needed. Uncle Nathan and Aunt Berthe would pay the cost of ship passage and meet the boat when it sailed into New York Harbor. It was settled. Oma and my cousins had a home waiting for them in the United States. We would travel together at first. Then they would go to the port of Marseilles and we would continue north to the city Papa had chosen for us, Lyon.

At five o'clock in the morning we gathered at the entrance, Papa on his feet with the rest of us. We looked at each other, aware that after a long recess we were presenting ourselves to the world again. What a comical assemblage we made. Our clothes were shabby and dirty. They were a few degrees better than rags. Papa's stylish cane with its round carved handle looked out of place, a reminder of better times. Five of us were wearing Maman's inventions - the knapsacks printed all over with large flashy flowers. Ridiculous! We could pass for a tribe of beggars. Despite the seriousness of the day, this was too funny. It was worth a laugh. Smiles were what we managed, except for Oma, whose mouth remained a straight line. Oma didn't smile a lot anyway.

The truck arrived. Papa and Oma rode in the cab with the driver, while Maman, Edith, I and the cousins steadied ourselves, standing and holding on in the open flatbed. We had, with variations, done this before. Gurs, the place, disappeared around the first bend in the road, to be replaced by Gurs, a peculiar dream, a memory.

We were on our way to the same train station where we had been put on trucks destined for the barracks and barbed wire at the edge of the Pyrenees. This time we were on our own and hungry for breakfast. It was August 16, 1940. The name of the depot was Oloron-Ste-Marie.

We went to the restaurant at the station, the Buffet de la Gare, but they turned us away. If we were once a middle-class family, the restaurant people couldn't tell. They said we should eat at a cheaper place, though nothing else was open. Before we boarded the train, Maman, Papa and Oma managed to get coffee. They drank it from cups, not the tin cans we used at Gurs.

We changed trains. Between rides we again tried the station restaurant. Again we found ourselves unwelcome. They sold us a little bread and chocolate which we took away and ate off to the side.

Our train pulled into Toulouse as evening fell. Time to test our luck at another restaurant. The staff tried to persuade Papa to direct his party of waifs to a building where refugees ate for free. Papa insisted he could pay. He succeeded in buying us potato soup.

The moment was coming when we had to part ways with Oma and my cousins. They were going on to Marseilles where they would await a ship that would take them to a neutral country. From there they would set sail to America, across the Atlantic. As for Maman, Papa, Edith and me, a midnight train would carry us in a totally different direction, north to Lyon.

We said goodbye at the station. I had no strong feelings. I was confused about where we'd been, where we were going, how long till we'd meet again. Not too long, I figured. I didn't at first sense the drama. There was Leon, oafish, ready as always to point out the low side of things. With him I wasn't in a hurry for the reunion. I would miss Lucie, but not painfully. She stood at Oma's side, the helper, companion, supporter of a difficult old lady. Oma was lucky in the arrangement, Lucie less so. She didn't complain. She had a simple good nature that not much bothered. But she wasn't sensitive or curious either and never spoke of having expectations for her life. Maybe that's how she was born to be. It didn't help that she'd grown up in the country among adults who thought only of practical matters, or that her grandmother, from the start, doted solely on Leon. Nobody would have tempted or prodded her to discover her true self. Except that he had Oma's special regard, the same could be said of Leon. To be fair, his childhood was as uninspiring as Lucie's. Being fair to Leon took effort. War had turned their world, whatever it was, inside out. Home and country vanished. Their father was dead. Their mother back in Germany had been lost to contact for months.

We turned to Oma. I had mixed feelings for her. I knew – had heard it many times – that despite her faults she'd been a lioness when it came to protecting her children. When Papa was injured she got around army rules that would have prevented her from staying with him and assisting in his care. Really, she pulled him through and he never forgot it.

But as a grandmother she played favorites. Each of her children had two of their own. In each pair, one was preferred. With Leon and Lucie, it was Leon. Lucie's kindness and Leon's boorishness didn't affect her choice. Leon was the boy and named, irresistibly, for her late husband. With Edith and me, it was me. I wasn't a boy, but Oma apparently allowed families one girl, and Edith should have known the quota was filled. And I had other qualities that Oma approved. She showed me how to knit and I caught on. Oma loved knitting. Edith demonstrated little interest and no talent for it. I was strong and independent. Edith was frail and full of problems. This might have brought out the maternal instinct in another grandmother – just not ours.

Edith disliked Oma, had felt this dislike from a very young age, and not because she wasn't the pet. I'm not sure she even thought about that. It may not have mattered if Oma liked her better. On a night when we still lived in Sarreguemines and our parents were out, Oma sat knitting in the living room. Though we were supposed to be sleeping Edith was looking at a picture book and talking to me. The sound of footsteps gave warning that Oma had decided to check on us. I lay quiet and closed my eyes. Edith continued turning pages by flashlight. When Oma arrived she gave the lights-out order in her usual bossy, scolding, expecting obedience manner. But Edith already had a tough, stubborn will. "Oh, go back to your knitting," she said. She was six. Oma couldn't believe her ears. She retreated without a word. From then on they mostly left each other alone.

Maman, the under-appreciated daughter-in-law, could have kept accounts on how she'd been treated. She could have easily decided to nurture resentments. No one would have blamed her. But she had always spoken to Oma with respect, and now the hour was late for remembering anything but good. She planted a farewell kiss on the old woman's cheek, our signal to do the same. Even Edith didn't have to be asked.

When it was my father's turn to say goodbye he crumpled into Oma's arms, sobs escaping all his efforts at control. A sudden heaviness filled my throat. Tears of my own blurred the scene. Papas don't cry. They are the ones, warm and solid, who make all hurts vanish. Why was Papa so upset? He would see his mother soon enough, wouldn't he? I would have done anything, anything to make him happy again. Maybe Oma wanted to live with us forever. I would have gone that far. I couldn't bear to watch him. This was so unlike the Papa I knew. I turned my eyes away as if they had trespassed.

When we last saw Oma and Leon and Lucie through the window of the train station, they were hurrying toward their hotel.

We went to find our train. Maman carried two valises and I had one, and all of us wore the knapsacks except Papa. He carried his cane on his bad arm, using his good arm for balance, his good hand to hold a railing when we went up and down stairs. There were many opportunities for stair-climbing in the railway station.

At midnight we stood on the platform. No haggard co-prisoners, no guards in sight. The train pulled in, grinding to a stop. No lettering, no signs declaring us the enemy. We were customers now. The doors opened and we entered one of the cars. No soldiers handing out tiny rations. No famished faces. No young women flirting for an extra slice of bread. We were the only passengers in our compartment. The engine started up. The whistle of escaping steam, the familiar smell of burning coal, the sound of metal moving over metal – all assured us we had left Gurs far behind. Lulled by the steady forward motion, eyelids weighted by sleep long postponed, we stretched out, taking more space than we'd paid for.

Gurs, with Dr. E. Chiszym, a
Polish pediatrician

Gurs, with a Spanish Captain

Gurs., August 1940: the entire family; standing Maman and Papa
Sitting: Leon Edith, Oma, Lucie and Renée

Chapter 12

Papa tried to hail a porter. Not that we had much to carry. We had come to Gurs with little and were bringing out the same. Well, not quite the same. We now had a wooden suitcase that a Spaniard sold us and, of course, the garish knapsacks. We wanted to walk and explore Lyon and even our few belongings would weigh us down. Wearing the knapsacks made us look ridiculous. We needed a locker. The porters would know where to find one but we couldn't get their attention. Despite Papa's gestures they hurried by. Finally my father made it clear he was offering money in advance, and a strong pair of arms gathered up our bags. We hadn't eaten since before boarding our midnight train and it was eleven in the morning. The porter advised us against the Buffet de la Gare. He was trying to shield us from a big bill, or more likely, from being turned away, a humiliation we knew something about. He recommended a small restaurant where the food was good and the prices reasonable.

We had our first sit-down meal as free people. I remember the cantaloupe dessert. Edith and I were eating it with such enthusiasm and must have looked so skinny that the waitress brought us second helpings.

We settled in a community adjoining Lyon. It had its own *mairie*, its own character, but pressed so close against the larger city that they shared a tram line. Villeurbanne had the tallest buildings I had ever seen. They lined street after street, reaching heights of twenty stories or more. I knew people had built them but couldn't imagine how. Today buildings go much higher but in those times and for me they well deserved their title: *gratte-ciels*, skyscrapers. Many of my future friends would turn out to live in the *gratte-ciel* section of Villeurbanne. Visiting them, I enjoyed riding the elevators. On some days, when the power was off to save electricity, getting to and from the upper floors was seriously tiring. Another downside of high-rise living was the occasional putrid odor. Garbage was incinerated in the basements. The elevator shafts carried the smell to every floor. But these were minor inconveniences compared to the fun of working the elevators and thrilling to the views - looking up from the outside and, from inside, down at the city.

The apartment Maman found for us was in a *gratte-ciel*, but a much shorter one. It was on the second of eight stories. (In France the second floor is called the *premier étage*, the first floor. The ground floor is the *rez-de-chaussée*.) Obviously, we had brought no furniture. The concierge helped us collect some pieces left by previous tenants. We hadn't brought much else either. But we were together. No one marched us about. We were a regular family again.

I entered the Ecole Anatole France. I was in grade four, Edith in grade two. As far as I could tell, we were the only Jewish children in a big school – the third in my nine years. Many families had moved here hurriedly from the Occupied Zone. Being displaced was almost normal. Being Jewish, a difference among differences.

The long-time residents were mostly working-class people who operated machinery, hammered, fixed, cleaned and sewed, drove trucks and trams. They displayed a certain confidence. The construction workers of Villeurbanne had built much of the town. Through their union they had ownership in the buildings they'd put up – including the astonishing *gratte-ciels*! No wonder they were proud.

At school we practiced handwriting as I had always done, aiming for a rigid ideal. The poems we memorized were longer than the ones from earlier grades. Grammar was becoming important. We were introduced to science, to the laws of elementary physics. We had history lessons about heroes like Vercingétorix, leader of the Gauls, taken prisoner by the Romans. We learned about Charlemagne's empire and the first French kings. Long and dangerous journeys to a place called the Holy Land were called the Crusades. There were battles with the Infidels, whoever they were. I never quite understood their purpose but knew that it was all very noble. When we studied geography, the teacher, Mademoiselle Donjon, concentrated on France itself. (In Longeville the year before – where we had "adopted" Gabriel, our soldier from Madagascar – we were learning about the French colonies.) Every two weeks we got to play games, run races and do folk dancing at a stadium away from school. We walked there in two rows, along tree-lined sidewalks, singing "marching songs."

I liked my teacher and classmates except for Monique, my rival for first place. She, too, came from northern France. Her blonde hair fell in long spiraling ringlets called English curls. She had brown eyes that seemed capable of burrowing all the way to where people kept their secrets. She recognized – I was sure – that my last name was uncommon. I believed she knew and it mattered to her that I wasn't French, not really French like she was.

When not hidden in her office, the *Directrice* commanded the halls and presided over assemblies. Her presence was exacting, severe. Fortunately, remoteness was also a quality the *Directrice* possessed. She had little contact with the students and seemed to keep aloof from the teachers. I remember only the first letter of her last name, C. And that *de* came between Madame and the last name beginning with C. It was aristocratic to have a *de* in your name. The *Directrice* was the only person I knew who was a *de* something. I think of her, when I do at all, as *Madame de C.*

After homework and supper it was still light. I would run across the street to the square. Children were always out between six and eight-thirty. We played hide-and-seek, taking cover behind the benches, bushes and fountain, crouching in the shadows of the buildings that formed the perimeter. We jumped rope, played tag and hopscotch. Most of us were nine or ten or eleven. Some were as old as fourteen. I remember Renée Caussidière and Madeleine – we called her Mado – and another Renée and the Raspal brothers, Jean and Claude. Claude was young, and wore short pants. Jean was a teenager and girls thought he was very handsome and suave. These children grew to be my companions. Their laughter and running footsteps filled the hours just before dark. I never got to know the others. They came and went. It was a time when people, uprooted from their original homes, were making their way to new places, settling down for short periods en route. My friends were the ones who stayed. I counted on them for a lively dependable society where school was forgotten and the realities that burdened adults denied entry.

The perfection of these early evenings was incomplete. Maman had decided that Edith should accompany me. My sister's French was good now. She had friends of her own. Why did they never appear when needed? Edith wasn't the most grown-up of seven year-olds. Her version of hopscotch allowed for jumping on the lines as well as over them and backtracking when she was supposed to travel straight ahead. This unusual hopscotch didn't catch on with anyone else. Soon I'd be called in to sort out the complications. None of my friends, I observed, had a small, stubborn, unskilled person hanging onto them. I tolerated Edith's company but wasn't pretending I enjoyed it.

Chapter 13

My father had always been proud of his ability to make a good living despite his handicap. Now he had no business to go to, no loyal employees, no income. Each morning he dressed in his suit and tie. After breakfast he read newspapers and wrote letters. He visited friends who had moved down from northern France and worried about relatives who were still in Germany. Occasionally money he was owed would arrive in the mail. He wondered about how long our funds would last. Despite his efforts to be and look busy, he was feeling unproductive. Even I could tell.

At the beginning of each month, men who smoked received coupons so they could purchase their allotments of cigarettes or loose tobacco. Bread, sugar, flour, milk and meat were also rationed. Each person was allowed a certain amount depending on whether he was a grown-up, a child, or an infant. Only men got tobacco. Papa was a heavy smoker. From the moment the coupons were in his hand he could see they weren't going to be enough. As his supply of cigarettes got shorter so did his temper. By the middle of the month he might have had nothing left. Maman, Edith and I collected his cigarette butts, combined the nicotine-soaked tobacco with chicory or weeds we found along the road, and rolled the mixture into new "cigarettes." Though our one-of-a-kind products smelled vile, Papa had something to reach for when his cravings struck.

Food rationing was a constant source of worry and frustration.

Having the right coupons didn't necessarily mean you would get your portion. There might not be enough to go around. Fabric for clothing, woolen knitting yarns and leather were also scarce. Most shoes were made with fool-the-eye substitutes for the uppers and wood or cork for the soles. Maman kept unraveling the dresses she had knitted for Edith, who was growing too tall for them and graduating into my castoffs. Maman used the yarn from Edith's clothes to make small garments for both of us – sweaters, scarves, hats. We also got outfits and shoes recycled from the older children of our parents' friends. It didn't bother me that I had few changes or that I wasn't in style. Edith felt it more. Though she didn't complain, nice clothes were important to her.

Once, Maman was able to get her a pair of new shoes. They could sometimes be found if you knew where to look. Edith's were of real leather, brown, with a good shine. She was transported to realms of delight. The first hours wearing them demanded her total attention. She would walk head down, eyes fixed on her feet. Without reminders to look outward she would have collided with a wall.

Maman left for the market as my sister and I were rising. There were days she stood in line for hours, starting long before we were up. Meat, fish, vegetables – queues formed for nearly every food. Maman knew she had to secure her position early. Supplies were often gone before reaching the last customers.

Only mothers did the standing, waiting and buying. Children were in school. Adult men didn't like to be seen on the street during the day, doing nothing better than holding a place in line. Policemen could be curious, asking, "What is your job? Where are you from? Where are your papers?" With so many people dislocated, transient, possibly fleeing from foreign authorities, the fathers couldn't predict what they might have to explain. A wrong answer could result in arrest. Mothers, it was understood, had to tend their families. In those days few women had careers.

Papa under any circumstances would have been discouraged from taxing his strength. Ever since suffering serious head injuries in World War I, he had been prone to seizures. Maman watched over him, aware of the stresses that could bring on these epileptic-type fits. Sooner or later he would have one. Then she would get upset, not trying to hide her feelings. If he was awake and we saw him begin, we would guide him to a safe spot. But usually it happened while he napped. Maman was afraid he'd fall off the daybed. He never remembered a seizure, but the brief storm in his brain often left a "souvenir." If no one was by his side to slip a small book between his teeth, he would bite his tongue. When he woke, the pain in his mouth told him exactly what he'd been through. And later, the slight distortions in his speech told us.

My father's condition didn't alarm me. He underwent these episodes so regularly during this period that I accepted them as part of life. I was more concerned about Maman. Everything and everyone seemed to rest on her. If she worried she rarely told us. But she did have a friend and maybe she shared her more anxious thoughts with her.

Maman and Tante Grit had bonded when they were teenagers in boarding school. Though Grit wasn't my aunt any more than she was Maman's sister, Edith and I had known her since we were babies – and "Oncle" Simon and honorary cousins Robert and Marcel. I was the same age as Marcel. We joked about being twins. Robert was older, artistic and sensitive. The two women took a genuine interest in each other's children. Tante Grit would ask me about friends and what I liked to do and kept track of my school accomplishments. She and Maman had only one kind of child – just boys or just girls. Having a friend produce the missing gender was convenient compensation.

Tante Grit had lived in Paris before coming to Lyon. Her elegant figure was attired in well-made clothes, the best she could afford and she could afford quite a bit. She had a long – though not sad – face, and piled her hair on top of her head, completing the fashion statement of "long." She naturally wanted Maman to be chic, and sometimes brought unusual garments or recommended a hairstylist, a dressmaker. Maman enjoyed putting herself together, but it was never her highest priority. She didn't bother with makeup except for a careful dab of lipstick. Grit possessed a talent for glamour. She was unique in our circle, the lady who without a doubt colored her hair. Red. That companies successfully marketed such a potion to customers who voluntarily applied it was a minor shock to me. Nothing grabs your attention like someone going out of her way to acquire what you already have and don't want. I reconsidered the low opinion I held of my own red hair. I wasn't prepared to reverse it but at least I glimpsed another point of view.

Tante Grit and her sons came to Villeurbanne before Oncle Simon, and stayed with us. Her affection extended beyond Maman and me and Edith to include Papa. Anyone connected with Maman was part of her family. Papa felt deeply responsible for his guests. He tried to care for the boys in the absence of their father. Robert got more than he bargained for when he came home late one night. Papa, sick with worry, flew off and slapped him as he walked in the door, apologizing with true regret in the aftermath. When Oncle Simon arrived a month – two months? – later, the four Epsteins – (that was their last name) – moved to a nearby *gratte-ciel*. Now if Tante Grit and Maman wanted to see each other, they would have to visit. Mostly Tante Grit came to us. She understood that Maman, even with her girls at school, was needed at home. It wasn't unusual for me to come back to the apartment and find that we had company. Grit, with her intriguing outfits, bright hennaed hair and equally strong opinions was as good an "aunt" as biology ever provided. Her sharp eye missed little. She must have noticed my mother's fatigue.

Maman was more tired than I had ever seen her. I didn't know why. She was very concerned about her father, my Opa back in Germany, but I thought there must be more to it. I couldn't have guessed that at times she was bleeding profusely. No one had explained menstruation to me. A few years later, she needed an operation to remove the large fibroid tumors that were growing in her and causing the heavy bleeding, a condition made worse by hours of standing in line.

I tried to help in small ways. I went to the *boulangerie* to buy bread. I got the newspaper for Papa. I tried to straighten our crowded rooms. I took Edith out with me. I registered her at school, went with her to doctors' and dentists' appointments. Her back hadn't grown straight as it should. I supposed – more than that, I was convinced – her posture problems came from slouching over, staring at her feet whenever she wore her new shoes. (No one else voiced this opinion which I kept to myself.) I accompanied her to the clinic in the municipal building for exercises and manipulations. Edith was always happy to be with me. I didn't mind when it was just the two of us. Resentment entered my head only when she interfered with the smooth progress of games with my friends.

Maman decided we should learn how to swim. Boys and girls wore the same black or navy one-piece suits. We got ours from Marcel and Robert who had outgrown them. The pool, called the *piscine*, was in the basement of the municipal building, the place to go for a vast array of needs. It had a theater where soloists performed and professional companies presented operettas. Under its one roof were doctors' and dentists' offices, the clinic where Edith got treated for her back, our swimming pool, some administrative offices and the residence of Monsieur and Madame Caussidière, the concierges.

At first we were scared, standing at the edge of what looked cold and deep and smelled strongly of chlorine. Edith seemed petrified. We each wore a big belt attached to a contraption outside the pool that would keep us afloat.

The lifeguard directing these operations never got wet. Few bathers were in the pool during our lessons. We didn't need to be embarrassed by our near nakedness and total awkwardness. We were lowered into the water and soon realized that we weren't going to sink. It didn't take long to master the breaststroke, the only style of swimming we were taught. Edith learned fast and quickly outperformed me. She had been afraid to put her head in the water. Now she was jumping in. She went from terror to bliss in record time.

The *piscine* wasn't open every day, fortunately. Edith would have tried to make us spend most of our free hours there. We went on Thursdays, a day without school. It was open on Saturdays but Papa didn't let us go swimming on the Sabbath.

When the lessons were over we invited our parents to come see what we had learned.

The large room was empty except for the pool. Papa's balance was uncertain and the damp tiled floor, slippery. The idea of swimming had always been strange to him. Before his army service he had been an athlete. Soccer and cycling were his specialties. He hadn't grown up around water. No one he knew swam. He must have been conscious that if one of his daughters faltered he could do nothing for her. Edith and I scampered to the dressing room. By the time we emerged in our suits someone had brought Papa a chair. Maman stood beside him.

I volunteered first, stepping carefully down into the water and wading out until I was chest high. From one side to

the other and back I demonstrated my modest mastery
of the breaststroke. After what I considered a respectable
performance I turned the show over to Edith. She leaped
into the pool, a mermaid returning to the waves. On her the
breast stroke looked like a ballet she had danced all her life.
She was no good at other sports – her curvature of the spine
prevented that. She didn't excel at schoolwork either. But here
was something she loved and could do with ease. I glanced at
Maman and Papa. They were watching, fascinated. Papa had
relaxed, a great smile on his face. He seemed to shed some of
his years and looked for a moment like a young man. Maybe
he was thinking about the playing fields, about a time when
his body was strong and graceful and obeyed his commands.
He had cast these memories aside, shut them away from his
everyday thoughts. Now a door had swung open. A child of
his, the delicate one at that, was showing talent and courage
in a sport he had never attempted.

When we were back in the apartment, Papa hugged Edith
with special tenderness. "I was athletic," he said, "but I could
never do this." At supper he murmured, "That little Edith … I
couldn't believe it!" We both looked a lot like our father, but
Edith favored him more with her very fair complexion and
pale strawberry blonde hair. For Papa, a part of himself had
been given unexpected life. This scene could have been hard
for me to witness. After all, I too had learned to swim.

There were times and places I'd been jealous of Edith, even
though she, not I, was often sick at home and struggling
at school. She seemed the center of my parents' devotion.

I would hear them praise her to people about some accomplishment, her neatness, even her less than adept knitting. She was the prettier child, I suspected, and she had the blonde hair. A few years later I confronted Maman.

"Do you like Edith better than me?"

"What?!"

"You never tell company about me."

My mother explained that life came hard for Edith. She needed extra support. For me it was different. I had success at school and many friends and no trouble getting on in new situations. And of course they loved me – dearly, every bit as much. This was an answer I think I knew, but needed to hear.

Today I wasn't envious. I was glad for my sister, as they were. Besides, I noticed an opportunity. After the evening meal, before the sun had set, I left Edith, Maman and Papa sitting around the table and opened the door to go and meet my friends in the square, alone.

Chapter 14

I'd never had the chance to settle anywhere for long, at least not since I was old enough to care. No sooner did I get used to a place than we moved. Maman and Papa and Edith stayed the same, but everything else shifted. City alternated with country. Relatives were close, then they were far. Climates changed, even languages. Faces and names vanished with each abandoned location. But this was the start of my second year in Villeurbanne. I was ten going on eleven. My friends in the square had begun to reveal themselves. Mado lived in a house with lots of brothers and sisters and a garden where her family kept rabbits. I was impressed by the numbers of new bunnies that repeatedly materialized. Claude, the boy from Paris, was sturdy and round in his knickers and sweaters, an avid participant in our games. He was actually my age but looked younger. I had a crush on his older brother. Jean only had eyes for Renée Caussidière, my best friend. I didn't blame him.

Renée C. was two years my senior. She had curves where I had angles, and she knew how to style her hair and walk with "attitude." She was aware, while I was innocent in a way that was feeling more and more like ignorant. She captured the group's attention with her easy command of slang. The words and expressions she used were novel to me and Edith. We found them intriguing but when we tried them out at home Maman didn't look at all pleased. Away from the crowd, Renée told me jokes she could barely finish without breaking up. I enjoyed laughing whether or not I understood the humor. Sometimes I laughed so she wouldn't realize I was clueless. Wherever Renée was it was fun to be. If Jean thought she was wonderful, so did I.

It can take a while to have a best friend. Renée and I managed it over the course of a year. In that time the sights and sounds of Villeurbanne had become sure and familiar. The shops and trams, the Ecole Anatole France, the *gratte-ciels*, the square that sprung to life every afternoon.

For my parents, the ground didn't feel so solid. Friends arriving from the German-occupied north told frightening stories. First individuals, then whole sections of a neighborhood were targeted. People were disappearing. Where they were being sent no one knew for sure. Rumors were circulating around about the *KZs* in Eastern Europe. KZ was pronounced *ka-tsed*, the German way. The letters stood for "concentration camp." None of us had forgotten Uncle Ernst, taken to one of the first KZs – Dachau, in Germany – never to return. These camps were not set up for large-scale murder, but as Uncle Ernst proved, it was easy to die in one.

If I had thought too hard I would have been terrified. My mind wouldn't let in the worst facts. What got in either wasn't understood or wasn't allowed to stay, or both. My school and my friends steadied me. And my parents were capable. They could handle any problem, no matter how big, I told myself.

Papa and Maman were busy "getting papers in order." What

that meant I wasn't sure except that they had to take papers to officials whose job it was to approve or not approve. When approval was withheld my parents had to get more information or take other measures to satisfy the official. Papers that were presented correctly got stamped, usually more than once or twice. One official decorated each piece of paper with about twenty-seven stamps, but only if it passed his inspection. His favorite phrase was *"Je n'accepte pas."* I do not accept this. Maman called him *Monsieur Je n'accepte pas*. She explained that he was one of a new breed of self-important men instantly promoted to positions of power because of the war. Such characters appeared to relish the difficulties they could create for others.

"Who is he, anyway?" Maman exclaimed, returning from a long, exasperating session. "He would be nobody if not for the strange times we live in!" She jabbed at an imaginary piece of paper with an invisible implement, saying, "Stamp, stamp, stamp, stamp ..." Then she collapsed into a chair. Her laughing mouth, gray-green eyes (one more gray, the other more green), and humorously tipped nose could not take *Monsieur Je n'accepte pas* seriously.

Papa's nerves continued to unravel. Worry about the war plus less and less money and less and less tobacco combined to keep him on edge. Usually kind and generous, he could explode suddenly over small irritants. Edith and I were going without the dolls we used to share. (They had been packed in the trunk that never made it to Gurs.) Maman scoured the secondhand stores and found us a replacement, a china doll with eyes that opened and closed. We cherished her. We would sit on Papa's daybed and move her through the scenes of our improvised little dramas. Sometimes we quarreled over who would be in charge of her longer, eventually resorting to language we had learned at the square. We were supposed to take the doll away when we were through playing, leaving the daybed clear for Papa. We didn't always remember. One afternoon he lost his temper. In an awful instant our treasure flew across the room and crashed into a wall. Her arm shattered. Edith and I gathered up the pieces. No one could console us. Papa apologized, shocked at what he had done. Again and again he told us he was sorry and soon I felt as bad for him as I did for the doll.

Maman visited another antique shop and brought home a celluloid doll's arm. She removed the broken china arm and connected the synthetic one to the shoulder. Our doll made a miraculous recovery, much to Papa's relief. Edith and I didn't care about her slight imperfection. Now the doll was more precious to us than ever.

Arguing with Edith I avoided if possible, if I was calm enough to remember the cost. It was hopeless to try to win and that wasn't because her reasoning was airtight. She didn't play fair. She countered opposition with whining, crying and insisting. No matter how little the merit in her viewpoint she wouldn't back down. Once the *Directrice* contacted Maman to say that Edith handed in an unusual amount of money to contribute to some patriotic cause. Perhaps Maman should check her purse. Sure enough, one large bill was missing. My sister wouldn't admit doing anything wrong. She tearfully maintained that she needed the money to show her classmates and teacher how much she cared. "I had to, I had to," she repeated. I knew Maman had a few choice words for Edith's whiny tactics, but in the face of this small "felony" she was quiet. Edith had suffered much in her few years with illness and language and constant change, with schoolwork that was too hard and friends that were too few. Maman allowed my back-against-the-wall sister to have the last word.

Edith's maddening blend of stubbornness, whining and wailing didn't make her popular among my friends. They called her a *pleurnicheuse*, a crybaby. But when real bravery was required the *pleurnicheuse* could be tough. I can see her, pale and still, her lips pressed together, in bed in the afternoon. The doctor had removed her tonsils. He'd performed the surgery on our dining room table with Maman assisting. Edith had submitted without a whimper when they put the ether-soaked gauze over her face. And when she awoke made no complaint. Not a sound, they told me, although with the anesthetic worn off, her throat would have hurt intensely. I trembled for my sister and imagined myself in her place, creating a pitiable spectacle. I had no talent when it came to pain.

The day before, Maman tracked down a store that sold ice cream, the best relief for tonsillectomy patients. French households didn't have refrigeration but the café/bar across the street did. My mother persuaded the owners to hold the special treat. Power outages weren't rare but the timing of this one was unfortunate. The ice cream melted before Edith could taste it.

Hop on one foot, jump on two feet, hop on one, jump on two, hop one, jump two …hopscotch was a game I loved. I completed my turn and handed the pebble to Mado who finished and passed it to a third Renée, Renée Morin, who at last transferred it to – oh no, Edith. After an ordinary beginning she reverted to her old habits. She dropped the pebble on the wrong square, turned around – stepping on the lines – retrieved it and would have continued had not Claude Raspal cried, *"C'est mon tour!"* It's my turn! Other voices joined him in support.

Edith tried to ignore the protests but this revolution wasn't going away. Children were on the court, pushing. Edith was pushing back. Time for me to do something. I took Edith by the hand and marched her to a quieter spot. "Let's play hide-and-seek," I suggested.

I persuaded some of our group to let her join us. We gathered by the fountain basin and closed our eyes, counting to ten while the designated person chose a hiding place. Figuring out where that was didn't take long. Shrubs, benches, niches in buildings – none provided complete cover. They soon gave up our quarry. A wicked thought overtook us when we were looking for Edith. Wherever she is, let her be. We regrouped at another part of the square. Someone produced a jump rope.

At last Edith appeared, furious. I tried, not very hard, to convince her we had searched everywhere in vain. Sobbing, she threatened, "I'm going home and telling Maman!"

I did my best not to smile at this welcome development.

"*Vas-y,*" I said, indifferently. You do that!

In a flash Edith was on her way to tell Maman the awful truth about me. A soft chuckle from the shadows announced the presence of Renée Caussidière. "*Quelle pleurnicheuse!*" she said. What a crybaby.

Chapter 15

Some people become friends because they are similar. Others are drawn together by their differences, like the poles of a magnet, like Renée and me. She was the south and I was the north. I had skin that burned in the sun. She had brown eyes and rosy olive skin and the rich dark hair I always wanted. I was reserved. Renée had a quick smile that lit her round, jovial face and a personality that tumbled forward. I loved a classroom, any classroom. My favorite gift was a book. Renée was an unenthusiastic student. She read what her teachers assigned, nothing more. Each day she waited for liberation from lessons and notebooks to come alive outdoors. She was twelve, two grades ahead of me. We struck up our friendship one evening in the square after supper. Only then did we find each other at school, in the halls, and during recess, in the yard. At noon and at four, when the doors opened and everyone poured out, we linked arms for the migration home. Renée and Renée. To distinguish between us, our friends invented variations on our last names. Renée became *la Coco*. I was known as *la Canne*. *La Canne et la Coco*, they called us.

On one of these after school walks she said, "Want to come with me and help my *maman* clean? It's fun." I would have agreed, even if cleaning the Caussidière apartment was what she meant. But she was talking about something different. Her parents were concierges, caretakers of the municipal building. They lived there, too, with Renée in a single room on the ground floor. Among their responsibilities was keeping the theater performance-ready. Madame Caussidière made sure that when patrons arrived, every trace of the night before had been swept away. Monsieur Caussidière was in charge of the ropes and pulleys, gadgets and electrical equipment backstage.

I met Renée and her mother in the large auditorium. Seats were attached like the pews in a church. There was a stage, a balcony and along the sides, the loges, compartment-like balconies for small groups and couples. Renée explained our job. The seats, which flipped up and down, were mostly down and had to be set upright. Then we'd be able to see and collect what was on the floor, staying alert for objects the theatergoers had forgotten. Madame Caussidière safeguarded the discoveries. If no one claimed them in reasonable time, the finders could become keepers – an energizing prospect.

Our investigations yielded candy wrappers and crumpled papers, abandoned programs, ticket stubs. Less common but of greater interest were scarves, ladies' gloves and embroidered handkerchiefs.

Renée was right – it was fun. Whenever possible I added my efforts to the Caussidière "cleaning crew." Soon I realized we were finding the best stuff in the loges – valuables like good wallets and binoculars. Aloud, I wondered why. Renée giggled. That was easy. The loges attracted lovers. With the hugging and kissing that went on it was amazing if these customers saw the show.

Items worth having didn't remain with us for long. Always, the owners turned up to dash our hopes of possession. We didn't care – that's not why we came. But once, wedged between two chairs, a green evening bag sparkled. Renée saw it first. From the yearning in her eyes I knew she wanted it. She said nothing. We handed it to Madame Caussidière.

Dressed in skirt, blouse and black apron, brown hair pulled tight in a bun, Renée's *maman* was a picture of unswerving right conduct. Her appearance sent a no-nonsense message. She had fine, regular features hinting at her earlier young girl self, but must have believed that at her age and station in life the time for frivolity had passed. Now her clothing was always dark, her face strong rather than pretty, the fine features maintaining their customary stern gaze. I was intimidated until I started to understand that she liked me. Without many words she made me feel approved of, even special.

We had permission to walk on the stage. I had been to the operettas with my mother and was fascinated by actors and costumes, music, make-up, lights – everything. For me the bare floorboards were magical, charged with the spirit of recent performances. Now here was something new – the prompt box, a hole in the stage from which discreetly delivered reminders could rescue an actor whose mind had gone blank. Renée pointed it out. Maybe she was afraid I'd fall in. I considered it a reassuring invention, in case I chose the acting life. (I, not my extroverted friend, imagined a career in light opera. After listening to me sing out, Tante Grit suggested I stick to dancing.)

Backstage was a jumble of props and sets. Vast paintings depicted blue skies, green forests, pink mountains, purple lakes.

I recognized the canals of Venice from a production of *Tales of Hoffmann* I'd seen with Maman. The canvasses hung from heavily weighted ropes. Machines, electrical wiring, flat plywood gondolas left over from the Venetian scenes, assorted planks and gears, loomed in odd clusters. Renée's father was master of this beguiling but dangerous wonderland. He didn't allow us to enter. If we saw him we'd run quietly away without waiting to be told. Of the Caussidière parents, Renée's *maman* was not the stricter one.

I must have seen him, the concierge of the municipal building, when Edith and I went to our swimming lessons and before that, when I took her for appointments with the physical therapist. He would have been around, the man with the keys. But until I knew Renée there wasn't a reason to notice. The first time he made an impression on me Renée and I were roller skating on the sidewalk in front of the building. (Neither of us could afford skates. We took turns with a pair Claude Raspal lent us.) He stepped from behind the big door, folded his arms in front of his chest and watched us. My idea of a father was someone in a tie and three-piece suit. Monsieur Caussidière wore a shirt and overalls and loose-fitting jacket – workman's clothing of blue denim. He was strongly built, with wavy black hair and tanned skin. Not since Gurs had I seen a man so unmistakably from the Mediterranean south. Renée glided by and his lips parted in a warm smile. A gold tooth caught the light. It didn't mar the beauty of his smile. Gold teeth were considered an asset.

As I resembled my papa, Renée resembled hers. It was evident that she admired him, enjoyed the fact of his charisma. Later I learned that they could clash. Their passionate temperaments were too alike.

The Caussidières lived across the square from me. Renée and I could see each other's windows. If I got to the square and she was missing I'd go tap on the glass. I'd watch as she kissed her *maman* lightly, vanished into the hallway and reappeared, pushing open the heavy front door. Then she would take my arm as we ran to join the others. I kissed my *maman* in the same formal way when I went out, but most of the time we were more like girlfriends. Renée and her parents didn't talk a lot. She didn't confide in her mother, as I did with mine. There was little joking across the generations. Monsieur Caussidière's smile was all the more luminous for being rare. I enjoyed my parents' trust. Renée seemed to be under surveillance. The senior Caussidières kept close track of her activities, checking from the window when we played in the square, calling her in early for this reason or that. She complied but made no secret of her annoyance at being interrupted. I wasn't sure why she merited such exaggerated attention.

Our class moved, all of us together, to the same room for grade five. I can't remember my new teacher's name, only that I felt safe with her. She was Mademoiselle Donjon's close friend. They both wore their hair short and boyish and dressed in very tailored clothes. They shared an apartment. I don't recall either of them ever being unkind or unnecessarily strict with us.

Monique and I continued our academic competition. She was first and I was second or I was first and she, second. I think I was ahead more. We never developed into friendly rivals. We exchanged few unofficial words and looked elsewhere when it was time to seek partners at dance or sport practice. She, who came from an old French family, regarded me with an air of detached superiority. Her dark eyes and pale blonde hair, unusual in combination, lent extra power to her aura. If she spoke to me her words were tinged with disdain, as if she were "on" to me. I didn't challenge her. I have to admit I let her undermine me. No one else saw it. With the rest I was confident enough. At the start of each month, when desks were assigned according to test scores, Monique and I must have looked equally favored – or nearly so – by the gods of schoolwork. Neither of us had to fend for ourselves in the anonymous gray of middle achievement. Or worse, occupy the last seat. That was claimed once and forever by Isabelle, an awkward, homely girl whose nose was always running. Her distance from the teacher ensured that she would never know what was going on. Her chances of catching up were nil. She seemed to own the last seat. It had been hers, uncontested, in fourth grade too. I was sorry for her, though I wished she didn't have to have red hair, the only red hair in the entire student population besides mine.

School had never been just about lessons and homework. From the beginning we participated in activities designed to stir patriotism. Our country had been at war or preparing for it since I entered grade one, which made these efforts more intense. We listened to stories and recited poems about *la gloire et la grandeur,* saw reproductions of French landscapes as interpreted by our great painters. Singing songs connected me with all my classmates, our separate selves dissolving into a warm ocean of good feeling. Folk dances transported us back in time past cities and automobiles. We could be pretend peasants in some deep original France of shepherds and farmers. My favorite dance involved holding a long stick, going under it or over it. You needed a partner and the teachers didn't forget Isabelle. They knew she wouldn't be chosen so they had her be first to choose. We were trained in *la politesse.* No one refused to dance with her.

In grade four, around the middle of the year, a new ritual had been added to our mornings. The whole school would gather in the courtyard to witness the tricolored flag go up while we sang, *"Maréchal nous voilà!"*

> *Maréchal, here we are!*
> *Before you, the savior of France*
> *We swear …*
> *To serve and follow your footsteps*
> *Maréchal, here we are!*
> *You have given us hope again*
> *The fatherland will be reborn.*

Suddenly, where nothing had been, portraits of Marshall Philippe Pétain appeared. From the walls of the corridors and classrooms he stared benevolently, like a noble, intelligent *grandpère.* He had saved France, Madame de C informed us in one of her pronouncements. We knew that from the song.

As fifth graders we were still singing the song and raising the flag. But that wasn't enough. We were now writing him letters and sending him money. On occasion, a bundle of mail would arrive at school, sealed envelopes addressed to each of us. The letters, copies of a handwritten note beginning, *Mon cher enfant*, told us to work hard for the sake of our country. They concluded with copies of the great man's signature. Opposite the script was a photograph of our hero on horseback, sword at his side, uniform bedecked with medals, on his head a kepi – a flat-topped military cap with a visor. We attached high significance to these messages, placing them carefully in folders to rest clean and smooth into the far future.

In keeping with the new spirit, every class had to have its own colors. Ours were red and green. We decorated our clothing with red and green ribbons for sports competitions and outdoor assemblies. We also had to decide on a class symbol. For centuries, the windmill – *le moulin* – had held an honored place in the French countryside, turning, turning, never idle. Since we were expected to be busy and industrious, it was an obvious choice. A poem about windmills by a famous writer provided the words for our class song. The Maréchal had written to us – to each one of us! – "Follow your tasks on a daily basis. You will serve yourselves and France." We were sure he'd like the windmill idea. We loved Maréchal Pétain. In the photos he looked as kind as my grandfather, my Opa who lived across the border. Opa hadn't written in a long time.

Young teenagers still played hopscotch, tag or jump rope at the square. They just didn't mix with the more juvenile groups. If Claude Raspal hadn't been one of our regulars we mightn't have got a good look at the older brother who stopped by for him. Jean's casual, unexpected visits evoked blushes and quickened heartbeats among the girls, including me. He was fourteen and from Paris, the center of the world. (Claude was equally from Paris but he was chubby and child-like.) Jean's manner seemed more elegant than anything we'd experienced outside of the cinema. He moved well in his clothes. He had chiseled features on a face of planes and angles. Next to him the boys our age were hopelessly infantile.

He didn't come often. Aloof, his thoughts to himself, nothing about him encouraged familiarity, and we girls of ten and eleven didn't have nerve to begin a conversation. We would have been tongue-tied if he had spoken. It was enough to look. And yet a negative note soon entered my estimation of him. He acted like he was far above us, like we were too small, too humble to exist for him, too babyish, too provincial. A few more of his forays in our direction strengthened my opinions. I told Renée, "Jean is stuck-up."

Her response was a surprise. "Not to me." Suddenly I understood. Jean had occasionally sauntered over on account of his little brother. When he stayed it was on account of Renée Caussidière. Why had I not seen? True, they didn't walk together. No visible gestures connected them. Except that Jean greeted Renée and nobody else. And there were the times I couldn't find her. She would disappear for twenty minutes, an hour. When she was gone, so was Jean. She reappeared. So did he. Renée's vanishing act happened only when Jean was in the vicinity.

If I was slow to add the signals, Renée's parents were not. One or the other would call out for her, cutting her evenings short. Renée smoldered. She would turn her back to the offending window and mutter words rarely heard and universally forbidden. (Books, magazines and movies in the 1940s followed strict rules of acceptable language.) Renée's fluency was unequalled among us and much admired, with slangy street talk. But these were syllables we'd never dare pronounce. She conjugated the five-letter "*m* word" – a noun turned verb – into phrases meaning "I've had it up to here with them," or "They annoy me." We were shocked. It was breathtakingly taboo.

When she was absent from the square – and it was happening more than usual – I knew she was in trouble. I wouldn't approach her window in case they were arguing. Instead I waited in front of the building. Sooner or later a Caussidière parent would come and say, "Renée has chores to do," or "Renée is being punished." Maybe news of her vocabulary had traveled.

Taking unprecedented measures, Monsieur or Madame Caussidière might march over and intrude on the whole group just to retrieve their child. Renée felt humiliated. Anybody would have. I remember her father taking her arm and how, as they crossed the street, she yanked it away. Once indoors, sounds of their angry voices escaped through the open windows. It wasn't the first time. At last Renée emerged, made her way toward us. Her eyes were red from crying and her cheek, too, where it had been struck.

My stomach turned over. I felt sorrow and a kind of embarrassment for her, that she had brought this on herself. I didn't condemn Monsieur Caussidière in my mind. A parent had certain rights. I'd learned many things, but criticizing adults wasn't one of them. I didn't question grown-up authorities – not my parents or anyone else's, or my teachers or the *Directrice* Madame de C., or the Maréchal Philippe Pétain who had saved my country, France.

Renée wouldn't rejoin our games. She held back, sullen and alone. I sidelined myself and went to her.

"*Ça va?*" Are you okay? Her face told me all I needed to know. Slowly and without speaking we walked around the edges of the square. We went first one way, then the other, not really noticing. But Renée could never keep a bad mood going. Not even at her most determined. The crisp air and the laughter of our friends were hard to ignore. The lure of running and jumping eventually proved irresistible. Renée's natural good spirits prevailed and we melted into the crowd.

A tap glanced my shoulder. "*La Canne et la Coco*, you're both It!"

Chapter 16

French schools closed one day in the middle of the week.
That was when Catholic children took their catechism classes.
To compensate for the time off, we were back at our desks
on Saturdays. The workload was light – finishing projects,
catching up on what we had missed. We were only there
half a day but school was school. By afternoon we were
ready for our reward. Once the family meal was eaten, Edith
and I headed toward the widest street in Villeurbanne, the
Avenue Henri Barbusse. Towering *gratte-ciels* lined the Avenue.
At ground level were the stores, the merchandise in their
windows arranged in an effort to make meager pass for plenty.
Above the stores were the apartments. An indoor hallway
connected the buildings. Nonresidents weren't supposed to
use it but on rainy days it provided the perfect shortcut. At
the end of the block the avenue was traversed by a long street
where trams ran. You could board one and be in Lyon in ten
minutes. Today we were going no further than the *gratte-ciel*
at the corner. Some of our friends would already have arrived.
Others might have joined us at various points along the
journey, turning a duo into a group. Soon we'd be settled in a
big dark room as full of children as the Ecole Anatole France
was now empty.

The dark enveloped us, united us in expectant silence. From
behind and overhead a beam of light shone. The floor sloped
down slightly toward the front so one row of heads didn't

block the next. The floor slanted but the light flowed straight out, illuminating a screen on which oversized people engaged in fantastic exploits. Along the light path particles of dust bounced and danced.

Sometimes we laughed at Charlie Chaplin or Laurel and Hardy, or saw operettas starring Nelson Eddy and Jeanette MacDonald. Most of all I loved stories about cowboys. We called them *"le far west"* movies, sagas of right and wrong that unfolded against stark, exotic landscapes. Edith and I seized each other's hands as the good cowboys charged over the hill to the accompaniment of the William Tell Overture. We held our breath hoping they'd succeed at the rescue – there was always a rescue – and sighed, our spirits restored when, at the last possible minute, the good guys triumphed. From the audible exhalation in the room I knew everyone was feeling the same thrill. (Some stories, instead of finishing, suspended the action at a critical juncture, making sure we would be back the next week.) The cowboys and Indians spoke French, which I accepted as natural. I had no notion that voices could be dubbed. Nor did I have any idea where the movies took place. The term *"le far west"* didn't register as a geographical location, only as an expression relating to cowboys or Canadian Mounties. The Nelson Eddy, Jeanette MacDonald operettas were also of *"le far west."* The words ran together in my mind – *lefarwest*. I didn't know that "Canadian" referred to a country though I did understand that a Mountie was some sort of policeman. Nelson Eddy always portrayed a Canadian Mountie and the action unfailingly included a pretty woman – Jeanette MacDonald. They too, spoke French, except for when they burst into melody and switched to an unintelligible language - English. The dialogue but not the songs had been dubbed, a fact that went right past me. I was unfazed because I'd been to the opera with Maman and knew that when people sang a certain kind of music I couldn't expect to comprehend the lyrics, even when they were in French.

A great advantage of attending the Saturday cinema was not being obliged to leave when the show ended. It would be played over and over. Having paid our several *centimes*, we could stay the whole afternoon. Watching the make-believe, I was safe. The world was distant. But between each showing of the featured film came *Les Actualités*, the newsreels.

There was Maréchal Pétain surrounded by children. They loved him and who could blame them? He had such a benevolent smile. He radiated kindness, like my Opa. They were much alike, I thought, except that le Maréchal was definitely older. The scene faded out and they were showing a map with lines and arrows. The map vanished and was replaced by footage of cannons blasting and soldiers running forward. A man's voice explained that things were going well for our German friends and for us, too, thanks to Maréchal Philippe Pétain, the savior of France. Next, the voice announced that a British parachutist had been captured. His picture appeared on the screen. We were supposed to feel victorious. Whenever the speaker mentioned Charles de Gaulle (leader of the Free French and after the war, President of France), he made it sound like de Gaulle and the

Frenchmen who joined him in England were traitors. German General Rommel, on the other hand, was to be applauded for his triumphs in Africa. *Les Actualités* usually concluded with lighthearted segments like the one about girls unable to buy silk stockings who solved the problem by drawing lines – "seams" – down the backs of each other's legs. No matter what, French women knew how to be chic.

Something was wrong. I had been trained to accept the words of adults. But which adults? We'd been fighting Germany, hadn't we? The British were on our side, weren't they? But the voice in the newsreel was cheering Germany on. The Maréchal had brought us quiet and order, it said, the results of the new harmony between the French and German nations. I didn't grasp politics but I knew we had fled Germany. Some of our relatives had left when it was possible, but not everyone. Not Opa.

At first I tried to shut out the contradictions. Shutting out had worked for me before and it might have worked now if I stopped going to the movies or the movies stopped showing newsreels. Neither was going to happen. Besides, I was getting more mature that year, more aware, whether I wanted to be or not. Madame de C. was always saying that le Maréchal had saved the honor of France, that he was "very good" for the country. There was no talk of defeat or compromise. I never made the connection that an agreement existed between us and the German enemy. Yet elements of normalcy were becoming apparent if you paid attention – like much less chaos in the distribution of coupons for food and clothing. I wasn't in a hurry to make connections, even as the newscaster threw the facts in my face. I did notice changes in my school, like the increased number of military-type, flag-raising, everyone-lined-up activities. I enjoyed wearing red and green ribbons. A lot of it was fun. But I knew adults called it "regimented." Not all adults approved of regimentation. The more cultured and educated an adult was, the less he seemed to welcome it. Come to think of it, my two teachers weren't that keen on le Maréchal, not nearly as much as the students and Madame de C.

I was affected by signs of suffering in my parents, especially when they listened to the stories going around about what was happening to the Jews in Germany and Eastern Europe. As the year went on, more refugees were coming to us for a meal, an overnight. Amid praises for Maman's cooking – they appreciated the simplest thing she served –; it was almost funny – they talked of "deportations" and "camps." I had been to Gurs, a detention camp. I wanted to forget it, but listening to them, I was forced to remember. Gurs wasn't as bad as these other camps sounded. It wasn't like we'd never heard of other, worse camps. We knew about the KZs. Back in Germany a member of our family had died in Dachau. And we knew that deportations had begun in France. Georges, the very nice sixteen year-old brother of the spoiled Henri (who started a shoving match at my eighth birthday party) had been picked up in full daylight on a busy street. Someone witnessed the arrest and told his parents, who still had no word from him.

Closer to home, *Monsieur Je n'accepte pas*, bureaucrat of the many stamps, was doing what he did best – refusing to certify my parents' papers until they produced information they couldn't find or never had. Maman's rheumatism flared regularly during this period. She would wait for me and Edith to come home so Papa wouldn't be alone when she went for massage treatments. The handsome, soft-spoken masseur was blind. He lived with his wife in the apartment at the corner of the hall, next to ours.

A movie opened in Villeurbanne, *Le Juif Süss*. I didn't see it but they showed segments on the newsreel. The main character, Süss, had a giant hooked nose and hands like claws. He was said to be evil. "Blood-sucking" was the term they used. An interviewer caught up with "average citizens" as they were leaving this movie which had caused a stir throughout the country. Yes, it was very good, very accurate, the filmgoers said, happy to be asked. The average citizens faded out, replaced by a group of angry-looking grown-ups carrying placards. They were Jews protesting the movie, photographed in a way to make them look rude and unattractive.

Surrounded by companions and schoolmates, I felt suddenly alone, a foreign Jew in France. I and my family had been imprisoned once for being foreign. Being Jewish seemed to be worse and I was both. Yet my teachers and friends didn't care that I had been born elsewhere. Nearly all the kids at school would be oblivious to my religion. Nearly all. Not Monique. She knew. I could bet on it.

The character Süss was utterly unlike anyone in my family or any of our friends. He didn't resemble anyone I'd ever met. But here were intelligent sounding voices saying otherwise. Could they be right? Were the Jewish people I knew exceptions? Was I? Nobody had taught me to recognize hate propaganda of the vilest sort.

My parents either went to the movie and were appalled or looked at the posters and were appalled. I can't say which. *Le Juif Süss* seemed to stay in town forever. After it left, the satanic-faced posters remained.

In the spring, before Passover, Papa was arrested. I wasn't home when the *gendarmes* came. Later I learned that they'd wanted to arrest Maman, too, but let her stay because of my sister and me. The twenty-four hours Papa was gone are a blur. I don't think I understood what had happened. He returned to us the next afternoon. I looked up and saw him in the doorway, pale and unkempt, as if he'd slept in his clothes.

The *gendarmes* had put him on a truck and driven him to a fortress in Lyon that they used as a prison. When they took him off the truck, he fell. Only then did they realize how disabled he was. Not being cruel men, they found him the only bed available. It was in the women's section and that was where he slept. The following day he was released. He didn't know why any more than he knew why he'd been arrested. Maybe *Monsieur Je n'accepte pas* had a hand in it. Now my father stood trembling before us.

Maman rose with a start. "Edmond!" They embraced with

their eyes and then for real, Papa murmuring, "Friedel, Friedel …" He drew back, looked at her, Edith and me, put his hands over his face and wept.

Opa had been living alone for a few years. His wife, my other grandmother – I think of her as the Oma of great dignity – had died in 1938. Maman missed the funeral because of travel restrictions to and from Germany. Later she was granted a visa and managed to pay her respects at her mother's gravesite and see her remaining family in Zülpich. Then, on November 9 and 10, 1938, Germany erupted in the government-encouraged anti-Jewish riots which came to be called Kristallnacht. The violence and destruction, the outpouring of hate even from neighbors formerly imagined to be friends, shocked Opa and Maman's brother and sister, Aunt Else and Uncle Joseph. They made plans to get out. Else and Joseph were cleared first. They immigrated to Brazil. Opa was expected to follow but something went wrong, a hitch in the paperwork, no one knows. Other relatives, too, were left behind. I remember the sadness in my parents' faces when they talked about it. I knew Maman was most anguished over her father. The bond was so strong. I felt that way for him too. He wasn't in his house, we learned from relatives. His business had been confiscated. We had long stopped receiving his drawings, the whimsical designs he used to create for me and Edith, or any mail that could have given us a return address. Released from Gurs, we were just setting up in Villeurbanne when it hit us: Opa was beyond reach. The year was 1940.

I was in fourth grade. I'd almost forgotten my bedtime prayer, the one I composed when I was seven. I never meant to stop talking to God. It was something I did and then didn't do. I wasn't disappointed because He didn't speak. I knew enough not to expect that. For vague reasons or no reasons my first attempts at prayer quietly dwindled. But in the last several months I'd experienced life in an internment camp. And more disturbing, our inability to locate Opa. Even my capable parents couldn't bring him close. If they were unable to help, I certainly was powerless. I decided to reopen communications.

The words came back to me, wishes that He bless Maman, Papa and Edith, relatives in general, Opa in particular, and my beautiful France. I updated my prayer with urgent specifics about Opa. Perhaps I should have listed all the relatives, like Oma and Leon and Lucie who had recently arrived in the United States, and Aunt Gusta and Opa's brother Otto and Otto's wife and daughters who were stuck in Germany, but I hungered only for Opa. It might sound improbable that his presence burned strong in me after years of absence, but it did. My other relatives were, in effect, consigned to the prayers of Maman and Papa.

Requesting heavenly intervention is serious. I substituted, for the first time, the formal *Grandpère* for the intimate German *Opa*. I considered *Grandpère* appropriately dignified besides being French, the language of the country I wanted to claim as my own, though by the middle of grade five my sense of security in this land was beginning to falter. After *Le Juif Süss* and Papa's arrest, stories of disappearances and the actual

121

disappearance of Georges, I couldn't deny the existence of unspeakable possibilities. The feelings I brought to my prayer intensified. The part about Opa always finished with, "May we find him safe." Holding fast to that idea I would sink into my pillow and let go of the day.

Not all my hours were clouded with worry. I was ten and then eleven and didn't know how to analyze the world. What weighed on me remained – as often as not – beneath a conscious level. Many things continued as they had in fourth grade and the beginning of fifth – friends in the square, teachers, friends and work in school. Renée didn't neglect to offer me tickets so we could attend shows at the theater. I recall the cabaret singer Edith Piaf performing. She was tiny and wore a black dress. She looked ugly to us. We thought her voice was horrible. Incredibly, the other listeners loved it. If this was supposed to be good, what objection could Tante Grit have to my singing, or anybody's? At least we hadn't paid for the tickets. More entertaining were the multiplying rabbits at Mado's house. We loved observing the antics of the new ones. Bunnies are expected at specific times, like in the spring. At Mado's they were arriving with far greater frequency. Her parents were mystified since the males and females resided in separate cages. Mado kept the truth to herself and selected confidants. As much as her friends liked watching the infants at play, she wanted to witness the mating rites of their elders and was mixing the sexes off-season. Mado was almost fourteen.

We didn't have a real Seder that Passover. We all remembered some fragments of the Haggadah and some songs. Somehow Maman had secured a box of matzo, and wine was always available. The symbolic sweet was a grated apple, and sprigs of parsley were the bitter herbs. It was easy to recreate the feeling of being unwanted in an unfriendly land.

Papa's recent arrest had dampened our enthusiasm for celebration, but the holiday was not ignored. My friend Renée had, of course, never tasted matzo, and when she stopped in to chat with my mother and have a snack with Edith and me, she got a chance to nibble on some "unleavened bread." I think she quickly understood my dislike of it.

Renée loved my mother, and found her occasional unusual French phrases charming. She was the only friend I invited to the apartment. I was totally at ease in her company. With others – I'm ashamed to say this – I would have been embarrassed by my mother's accent. At home with our family I hardly heard it. Only among my friends did her incomplete grasp of the language and German tinged inflection make me uncomfortable. I suspect that hearing her in the company of the native born disturbed my vision, no less cherished for being imaginary, of belonging a hundred percent to France.

I remember my first visit to Renée in her apartment. If a person had cause to be self-conscious, she did, living with her parents in one room. They weren't, after all, stopping at a hotel while on vacation. This was it. The couple's bed was screened off for privacy, but a screen hinders view, not sound.

Whatever they said to each other that they didn't want Renée to hear would have had to be whispered low. Maybe her ears were absorbing more than was intended for them. The jokes that I didn't get, for example. Renée gave no sign that she considered this arrangement inconvenient or extraordinary. Lack of an in-flat bathroom didn't faze her. When I asked to use one she directed me to the public facility on her floor. She felt no embarrassment about her modest home; she preferred the outdoors anyway.

The weather warmed up. Outdoors was also where I wanted to be. I had a great hand-me-down. Not clothes or shoes. Not a bathing suit. *Une trottinette* – a scooter! It was gray-blue, the color of the bike I'd wanted but never got. It had come to me in the fall, courtesy of Marcel and Robert. Edith showed no interest in my new means of transportation. Lucky for her, since she wasn't going to be allowed on a contraption capable of tipping over. I took it out all year, in winter, too, unless there was rain or snow. It had a pedal in the center of the platform where I stood. I could push it up and down and achieve real speed. With the arrival of spring we hardly missed a day, my *trottinette* and I.

I sailed to the newspaper store for Papa where, every two weeks, they sold a girls' magazine – *Marie-Coeur*, with its cartoons, jokes and stories. I bought bread for the family at the *boulangerie* with our coupons. If I forgot the coupons I didn't leave empty-handed. They knew me. I rode to the *bibliothèque*. It was so close to home that I developed a roundabout route, rolling effortlessly over the flat sidewalks past the *gratte-ciels* and the private houses with their gardens. At the library I borrowed books with my own card. If this was independence, I was going to like it.

The *trottinette* had no lock. We didn't worry about people stealing. I thought nothing of leaving it undefended for the few minutes required to complete an errand or longer if I was browsing in the library. At the end of an outing I maneuvered it up the stairs to our apartment. Wheeling it through the corridor I might encounter Monsieur I-never-quite-caught-his-name, the masseur, coming from his rooms. He would walk carefully, holding the wall. He recognized my step as surely as a sighted person knows a face. "How are you, Renée? How is Maman? Papa?" He didn't keep his eyes closed like some blind people do, or wear dark glasses. He simply looked ahead, eyes trained forward as if toward a pleasant view. He had straight black hair and was Mediterranean in appearance like Monsieur Caussidière. More educated than Renée's father, he spoke a beautiful French with only the slightest accent, either Italian or Spanish. Something about him reminded me of the men in the infirmary at Gurs. His age was the same – mid to late thirties, though a child can't be certain. His gentle, almost musical voice, his looks and bearing, made me think of the disabled veterans reading, listening to each other. That he was blind raised the possibility of a connection. Maybe he had joined one of the foreign regiments that fought on the other side of the mountains, in Spain. Maybe he was wounded in battle, lost his sight. Maybe he was Spanish. Of course I didn't ask.

On a mild, inviting Sunday, Maman, Papa, Edith and I might board the tram for Lyon, for a promenade in La Tête d'Or, a park that was also a zoo. The paths of this lovely park made for comfortable strolling that did not tax little sister or Papa excessively.

La Tête d'Or had masses of vivid flowers, such as petunias, begonias and pansies. In one section they were planted to form the emblem of the city of Lyon. Aviaries held falcons and eagles, geese and bright plumed pheasants. We could peer through the bars of cages at monkeys, lions and tigers, and marvel at their behavior and interaction. *What do they think of us?* I wondered. There were enclosures with odd-looking cows, some zebras, deer and giraffes. One section had an exotic cactus and succulent garden.

The grass was off limits but benches dotted the walkways. You didn't want to come here hungry. There were no restaurants or cafés in the park. Maman would search her bag and discover, as if by magic, an impossible luxury: a bar of Côte d'Or, a thick creamy chocolate. She'd break it into three pieces – for Papa, Edith and me – pretending she'd already eaten hers. Chocolate was more than candy. It was food. We would pile on a bench, savoring La Côte d'Or at La Tête d'Or. Of course, there was usually some seasonal fruit, the one food that was not rationed in this rich part of France.

Villeurbanne had a park, too, near the square, behind the municipal building. It was very small. Roses were the only flowers. A few statues, serenely gesturing, decorated the green.

126

They weren't as good as the ones I remembered from Opa's shop. I saw the Caussidières in *Le Jardin de Roses*. They might have been coming from church, the way they were dressed. I was alone. If Maman and Papa had been with me, Renée and I could have introduced the adults. I would have liked to bring our separate worlds together if only for a moment. Close as we girls were, a stone's throw from each other, close enough to signal from our windows if we'd wanted to, our parents had never met. Not once. Not even to say hello.

Chapter 17

It was June, 1942. Days lengthened. The air turned muggy and hot. No one had energy. My friends and I left off playing tag and jump rope and settled for winding string around our hands – cat's cradle – or folding paper to fit our fingers so we could tell the future. The streets were filled with refugees on the move. Despite the heat and humidity there were more of them than ever.

The presence of so many strangers – identities, purposes, and politics unknown – worried the parents. A young man in his twenties was making himself into a pied piper. He had a personality that drew children in. We had nothing better to do than gather round and listen to his stories. Some of us, including me, sat on his lap. When the parents realized what was happening at the square, they began to keep the children home after school. The young man might have been a recruiter for the *Compagnons de France*, an organization modeled on Hitler Youth. Perhaps Villeurbanne, a socialist stronghold, wasn't providing enough junior converts to fascism. On the other hand, he could have been a Resistance partisan. Or something less admirable. Or nothing at all. Our parents were taking no chances.

During the final weeks of school we wrote our exams. I wasn't forced to cram since I'd been keeping up. I was already looking forward to next year when I would transfer to the *lycée* and begin a curriculum that would prepare me for university.

Children were channeled early into academic or vocational tracks. Those who continued at Anatole France would graduate at the end of eighth grade and go on to a vocational school. They would get a thorough high school education and also learn a trade. People with trades could earn good money, often more than university graduates. With me the direction of my studies had always been clear. What I would do when I grew up was less certain.

I liked to imagine some kind of medical work. Maman had a gift for nursing which she almost pursued. Maybe I would discover similar abilities in myself. Nursing in a far-off land would be exciting. I'd heard of a doctor, Albert Schweitzer, who'd gone to live in Africa and founded a hospital to care for people with leprosy. Or there was art. I loved to draw. Opa was good at it. We had talent in the family. But then, Tante Grit said I should stick to my dancing. All these choices were confusing. I was glad I didn't have to decide yet. At least I'd given up on singing, which helpfully narrowed my prospects. Edith loved the thought of homemaking – cooking, tidying, looking after children. I couldn't muster enthusiasm for any of those activities. I supposed I'd do them when the time came, but as fantasies they were totally inadequate.

One aspect of changing schools made me sad. Leaving Renée. I reminded myself that we had the square and our nearby apartments.

On the last day of school there was still no break in the weather. I felt unusually light and calm that morning though the sky was gray and the damp warm air made our dresses stick to our skin. Madame de C. had brought the entire school out to the courtyard. We stood in lines according to our classes. She had an announcement to deliver. They liked making us guess. Well, I could guess it was about prizes. My heart didn't pound. There was no catch of suspense in my throat though I knew I was in the running. I didn't care a whole lot. For me, learning was the thing. Whatever she said, whoever she named would be okay with me. So I thought. Nothing could have steadied me for what was to come.

Yes, there was a prize. A lucky girl would receive a book about the life of Maréchal Pétain, a present from the great leader himself. Madame de C. went on about the virtues the Maréchal was seeking in his winner – excellence in scholarship, excellence in sports, excellence in sportsmanship. Sportsmanship. That was really something, to get along with your teammates and rivals, to win and lose with equal grace. And who was this paragon? Renée Kann. Me! She had said Renée Kann, but wait. Now she was saying not Renée. And why not? Renée belonged to a troublesome group of people. A race that caused problems for France. What people? But I knew. I was Jewish. *Les Juifs. Le Juif Süss.* That's who I was. When she said this group, this race, had been harming the country, she meant me. Harming my country. That was the worst part. The *Directrice*, the children in their lines, the old building, began to swim as my eyes filled with tears. Madame de C. was redirecting the award. I didn't follow Monique's progress as she moved forward to collect her book, or see if her long hair shone even under sullen clouds, or notice if she flung me a quick, smug glance meant for the two of us alone. By this time I had pulled my apron up over my face and was sobbing uncontrollably. My teacher and Mademoiselle Donjon from grade four tried to comfort me but I wouldn't be comforted.

I was still crying as I cleared my desk and hurried toward home. Edith was beside me straining to match my pace. Was she crying too? Did Renée Caussidière find me and put her arm in mine? *La Canne et la Coco.* I don't remember, but she must have been there.

I was rescued from having to face my friends the next morning. Instead, Maman took Edith and me to a section of Lyon we'd never explored, the ancient part of the city, set on a hill. I knew the name of it – La Fourvière – and that it was on the other side of the Rhône River. The tram didn't go there. We walked across a bridge and up the hill. Maman didn't know the area so we stopped often. She consulted her directions while Edith and I looked around at gray attached buildings on either side of gray cobblestone streets – narrow, winding streets that met at crazy angles, creating intersections where you'd least expect them. By method or luck Maman got us to the right address. We climbed the stairs to meet the lady we had come to see.

Our visit went quickly. Edith and I waited while she and Maman huddled in earnest conversation. She looked our way with a grave but friendly smile and let Maman know the answer was yes. She seemed tall to us and wore her hair

in a chignon. Her name was Madame Dreyfus. She would
be taking us to the mountains, Maman explained on the
way home. We would be staying in the region of the Massif
Central. No, Maman and Papa couldn't accompany us
this time.

The Massif Central. We'd learned about it in geography class.
It was one of the oldest mountain ranges in France, born of
erupting volcanoes. Robert and Marcel went there on ski trips,
to Mont d'Or, a holiday destination. The plan was for us to
meet Madame Dreyfus early tomorrow. Great. Another day I
didn't need to worry about facing anyone. And then I'd be off
to a famous mountain resort.

We packed the same evening: underwear, socks, a toothbrush
and toothpaste, a washcloth and half a bar of soap, an
extra sweater, handkerchiefs, a nightgown, and for me a
special treasure. Maman had made it as part of my class
requirements. Using cardboard and cloth she had sewn a
small bag that fitted neatly on a belt. Inside were gauze and
tape, a little pair of scissors and a mini-bottle of iodine: my
own first aid kit. Once, in another place, I was entrusted with
a pocketknife and taught what to do in case of snakebite. Not
since then, since my short membership in Les Guides, did I
feel so capital R responsible. My new *Croix Rouge* (Red Cross)
kit filled me with pride.

We put our belongings into knapsacks. Not the flowered ones,
I noted with relief. Just the ordinary type of a dull, dark, solid
color, pre-owned by Robert and Marcel. At least my entrance
into ski country wouldn't have to be a comic event.

132

When we were dressed to leave, Papa was in bed opening his eyes. Edith and I planted small kisses on his nose and forehead. *Au revoir, Papa.* Maman prepared bread and fruit preserves for breakfast. We ate little, said little. Outside it was dark. Maman added a peach and grapes to each of our knapsacks. My eagerness for this trip wasn't holding. A tight knot that started in my stomach reached up to my throat and spread down through the top of my legs to my knees. The four of us had never been separated for long. We'd survived everything sticking together. It was the sticking together that did it, I thought. Maman was anxious. I could tell but didn't say anything. Edith, clear-eyed, absorbed in anticipation, was happy as always to be going somewhere with her big sister. And Renée, the one friend I was unafraid to face – when would I see her? It was too early to tap on her window.

Maman took the streetcar with us to the train station, the Gare Perrache. A few sleepy people heading to work in the faint light shared our ride. For a change the air felt chilly. I was cold but maybe it was more than the weather. Maman reminded us to be polite, to look out for each other. Of course the families we were going to would be glad to have us. No, she could not visit. She wasn't sure how to correspond but we would have each other. We didn't have a phone in our apartment and we couldn't count on access to phones in the mountains. Of course Madame Dreyfus would have Tante Grit's number. I wanted to speak but didn't trust my voice. I knew I was expected to act brave.

The tram stopped at the station and we walked to the

platform. Madame Dreyfus was waiting for us. I didn't see any children with her. Somehow I had thought there would be other children. She was dressed severely, her hair pulled up under a black hat that made her look older than she probably was. But her smile welcomed us and she put her arms around our shoulders. She signaled to my mother to make the *au revoirs* brief.

We boarded an imposing train that had numerous cars but not many passengers. We had a compartment to ourselves, Edith and I on one bench, Madame Dreyfus across from us. Edith snuggled against my side and relaxed to the rhythm of wheels and engine. Whenever Maman was absent she transferred her confidence to the next best thing, the big sister. I didn't mind. I knew the role by heart. We passed factories and drab, flat, industrial spaces. Then some green, but no mountains, few fields, nothing unusual. Madame Dreyfus didn't try to make conversation.

I knew the Massif Central was somewhere west of Lyon. I couldn't tell what direction we were going, only that we went one way for a while, then changed course.

We disembarked at St. Etienne and sat on hard wooden benches amid the disorder of a large, busy railroad station. Over the loudspeaker a voice announced trains leaving from various platforms, none of them for us. We ate our peaches, played cat's cradle and kept quiet. We checked the contents of our knapsacks with care, especially my little Croix Rouge kit. The wooden bench grew harder – I was convinced – the

134

longer we sat on it. *We didn't take much,* I told myself. *We'll have to come back soon. I'll tell Maman and Papa about our adventures. And Renée. I'll surprise Renée.* Suddenly Madame Dreyfus told us to load our knapsacks, took each of us by the hand and steered us to a particular platform. The train to Le Chambon was leaving from there.

This train was short, unimpressive compared to the first. It moved slowly, belching quantities of heavy black smoke. As soon as we were clear of St. Etienne it made loud train noises as if to declare, now we are on our way. The views turned rural. Above, sun and clear sky and any moment, I was sure, the mountains. I decided it was time to share what I knew with Edith. I summoned to mind all I'd been told about the Massif Central. Without a lot of information I was building it up and Edith was taking it in. At some point my descriptions must have become too much for Madame Dreyfus. I had a few details wrong. For one thing, we were not going to the ski resort. Our destination was an agricultural region. The people who would be our hosts were mostly farmers, poor farmers, for the soil wasn't rich. We were going to live on a plateau, which is elevated. There would be some small hills, but definitely no mountains.

Oh.

The distance from St. Etienne to Le Chambon is about the same as from Lyon to St. Etienne, but this leg of the journey felt longer, maybe because we stopped so many times. Again and again Edith and I thought, *This is it,* but Madame Dreyfus held us back. The train seemed unable to travel a straight line. There were curves and more curves and uphill climbs through forests and over fields of grazing land. We saw cows and goats and – this was the beginning of July – patches of poppies growing along the tracks. The open window let in the sulphurous smell of burning coal. Tiny specks of soot floated in the air, tickling our eyes and noses.

Madame Dreyfus leaned toward us as if to impart the most casual advice:

"Ecoutez, mes enfants. When you get there, when you meet people, don't tell them much about yourselves. Not your religion or the country of your birth or that your parents live near Lyon."

Part Two

The Habit of Guarding

Our Tongues

Summer to Early Fall, 1942

Chapter 18

I woke with a start. The noise came again, making the wall shake. I was the only occupant of a bed big enough for three or four girls my size. It was tucked in an alcove and I was right next to the wall from whose unseen side the strange banging originated. If any thought was in my head this early in the morning it was, *Where am I?*

We had arrived late in the afternoon two days earlier. Our slow little train – our *tortillard* – pulled into the station in front of a sign that read *Le Chambon sur Lignon*. We walked a short way to the home of a lady called Madame Déléage. A man was waiting there. Madame Dreyfus seemed to recognize him. She didn't introduce me but motioned for Edith to take his hand. My little sister would be going to live with the gentleman and his family, though nobody spelled this out for us. I hugged her, not understanding that we were really going to be separated. Edith was equally unaware. She left with a brave smile, probably expecting to see me the next day.

I spent the night with Madame Déléage, whoever she was. In the morning Madame Dreyfus reappeared to escort me to my host family. A horse-drawn cart conveyed us through areas of forest with tall ferns growing on both sides of the rugged path. By early afternoon we had reached a small farm set alone on a hillside with nothing to disturb it from any direction – no other buildings, no stores, no neighbors, no traffic. Just the silence that makes you notice sounds of birds and leaves.

There was a trough with a pump in front of the house and a tiny vegetable garden in the back. It was a rough gray stone house with a bright green door.

The door opened onto a kitchen which was also a living room and dining room. An alcove hewn into the back wall held a bed. Only Madame Fournier was at home. She and Madame Dreyfus talked while I went outside again and looked around. I had traveled far to come to … nowhere. They called me in and Madame Fournier showed me a place to put my things. The pump in front of the house was where I could wash – myself and my clothes – and fill a cup when I was thirsty. There was an outhouse behind the stable. The stable was empty, but not for long, I was told. Madame Dreyfus prepared to leave. She promised to keep track and ensure that I had everything I needed. Yes, she would check on Edith too. No, I couldn't correspond with my parents. Seeing my face she added, well, maybe on occasion I could go to Le Chambon, where they had the post office.

Madame Fournier wore a gray blouse and black skirt under a gray apron. Her clothing was severe but her manner was pleasant toward me, on that first day and all the time that she sheltered me.

Near evening Monsieur Fournier and nineteen year-old Marcel returned. The elder Fournier must have met up with his son, who was bringing a whitish cow and a brown goat in from the fields. The animals drank at the fountain and went to their stalls. *So that's who lives in the stable,* I thought.

Marcel smiled and said hello. He reacted without dismay to the news that I'd be taking over his alcove. I wondered where he was going to sleep – a question that remained unasked and consequently unanswered. But a door led from the kitchen to a room I never entered. I assumed it was the parents' bedroom and Marcel would now be sharing it.

Monsieur Fournier wore a black beret, black stained pants and a sweater, even though it was July. One sleeve of the old sweater hung limp. He had lost an arm in *La Grande Guerre*. "*Les Boches,*" the Germans, had done that to him, he said – and I felt immediately responsible. Nobody needed to tell me to keep to myself and not speak about my background.

We ate our dinner sitting on wooden benches at the wooden table. I hadn't eaten since breakfast at Madame Déléage's but was too shy to admit my hunger. Madame Fournier served string beans, pieces of lard and homemade goat cheese. The clean air, the high country setting, gave each bite extra flavor. She urged me to take more but I refused. I'd been taught that, as a guest, I mustn't accept second helpings.

Afternoon retreated and with it, the light. The kitchen was dark anyway, with a dark dirt floor, one window, no electricity, and smoke from the wood-burning stove to fog our vision. I helped clear the table and wash the dishes at the pump. The family got ready for bed. One more look at the animals, one more visit to the outhouse and everyone retired. I hid under the covers – they had been Marcel's covers the night before – and undressed. I said my prayers, asking God to watch over my parents, make sure Edith was all right, and please, please, send *Grandpère* to us soon.

At night the only thing to do was go to sleep. The bedding wasn't fresh but at least there were no bugs. I slept until dawn when the strange thumping began. Later, the mystery was solved. A wooden partition separated the kitchen and my alcove bed from the stable. Gentille the goat, impatient to be milked and fed, was knocking against it, butting it with her horns. In case this wasn't enough to banish sleep, a rooster crowed. So, somewhere was a chicken coop. That was a detail I had missed.

Chapter 19

Madame Fournier came in as I was putting my clothes on under the covers.

"Bonjour petite. Tu as bien dormi?"

"Oui, merci." Yes, I slept well. I asked permission to wash at the pump. The rest of the family was getting ready for breakfast without benefits of the pump. They took turns visiting the outhouse and – I noticed – went straight to the table. On his way, Marcel stopped, arrested by the sight of me brushing my teeth. He called both parents to come and watch. They had never seen a toothbrush.

We ate thick slices of bread with sweet butter and jam. I was offered milk but drank water instead. I never liked milk. I tried to follow the conversation. It took me a few minutes to realize they were speaking a language I didn't know. I felt odd and left out. Maybe they were saying things about me. In fact they were just being themselves. It was natural for them to use these words, their everyday words that they might have assumed I understood. In their world, everyone did. I was hearing the ancient sounds of Auvergnat, a dialect related to Provençal.

The morning passed, slow and quiet. We washed the dishes. Marcel cleaned out the stable. I helped Madame Fournier feed the chickens. Hello, noisy rooster. We did some gardening – picking weeds, looking for slugs and the wrong sort of insects, finally plucking string beans and pulling up carrots. I loved the smell of the fresh vegetables. When we finished I went in and straightened my bedding, then back through the green painted door to give my surroundings another chance. There had to be farms – a farm – nearby. Up and down the dirt road I walked, casting my gaze north, south, east, west. No sign of human habitation.

For lunch we had string bean omelets with a slice of bread for each of us. Monsieur Fournier was absent. He had gone into "town." Without him I could better enjoy the food and the company of Madame Fournier and Marcel. I was comfortable with them. And when it was only the three of us they spoke plain French.

After the noon meal I went with Marcel and the animals to the meadow. It was the same each day, a rhythm I could depend on: Marcel and I, Gentille the goat and Pêchette the cow, starting at the low hill behind the house, climbing up and over it, then through the stretch of shrubs and trees that opened to a meadow. The land descended gradually to meet a brook alive with sparkling, cool water. Water in motion. Young men stood around talking while their animals grazed. So we weren't, after all, the only people for miles.

Marcel got in on the conversations. He made no effort to introduce me. None of the young men asked my name. They hardly seemed aware of my presence. An extra goat in the field would have stirred more curiosity. Well, I wasn't interested in any of them either. My indifference matched theirs. I climbed down to the brook, its gurgle becoming louder as I approached. The water ran clear, revealing the pebbles that rested just beneath. I collected them, brown and white, and arranged them in patterns. They were as beautiful as flowers. As for actual flowers, I didn't see many – maybe it was the wrong time of year – only interesting berries on some of the shrubs. I considered turning them into necklaces but that would require a needle and thread. Too bad. I looked at the forest that began on the other side of the brook. Among the trees were ferns like the ones I'd noticed along the narrow, bumpy road from Le Chambon to La Souche, ferns taller than I was.

Cautiously, I stepped onto the large stones that sat firm while water rushed past and wavelets lapped at their sides. Our little stream was quite shallow. I reached the opposite bank without getting my feet wet. At once I felt the power of the forest, even this one, not of dense pines, but of leafy trees that admitted more sky and light. I examined the ferns. *If they are cut I can weave them*, I thought, and resolved to make a basket.

I tried to break one of the reed-like stems, stabbed at it with my fingernails. Impossible. I stripped away the fronds, pulled the stem, and the whole plant started to loosen, roots and all. No, I didn't want to do that, didn't want to kill the fern. Marcel came looking for me. He was puzzled by what I was attempting, but, good-natured, used his knife to cut some ferns, as many as I wanted. My arms filled to capacity, I followed him back across the stream to the meadow. I removed myself from the others, sat cross-legged beside my heap of raw materials and would have begun weaving my basket when I realized I had no idea of what to do first. A basket needs a flat base. How to make that? They were watching me. I was sure. Invisible antennae on the back of my neck registered the scrutiny. I had confirmed what the young shepherds must have all along suspected. Here was a city girl who understood nothing of Le Chambon, nothing of life on the plateau.

The deep slant of the sun's rays announced late afternoon. The shepherds rounded up their animals, driving them in different directions to their homes. No one took our path. Pêchette and Gentille needed to be milked. That didn't stop Pêchette from stalling, diverted by a fragrant tuft of grass. Marcel hit her on the back with his stick. I cringed at the sound. The cow resumed her homeward progress, showing little reaction to the blow. But her mild gaze, itself a rebuke, seemed to say, "I just wanted a moment more with the lovely grass. You didn't have to get excited."

After Gentille and Pêchette drank at the trough, Marcel and his mother milked them in the stable. The goat milk was set aside for cheese-making. The family would keep some of the cheese; the rest would be for sale. The cow's milk was also divided – some for home, some for sale. That explained Monsieur Fournier's trips into town.

On the first Sunday – a special day, I could see – everyone got washed at the pump. It was a thorough exercise which didn't neglect even feet. Except for one practice, I would have found no fault in the all-family clean-up. The towel they used for drying feet was used next to dry ripening goat cheese. Ugh!

At the start of the second week Monsieur Fournier returned from town with news. Hundreds of British bombers had hit Lyon. There had been heavy damage to the city and many casualties. He had heard all this, he said, at the local café. I was filled with fear for my parents.

The next day I set out with him on the hike into town. First we went to the meadow – the same meadow where Marcel and I watched the animals – then down to the rippling water and over the pathway of stones, our bridge to the far side of the brook. We entered the forest and continued on, deeper. It wasn't very dark. We came out into another meadow and kept going, crossing two highways. The walk was moderately long. It felt longer since we exchanged no words. None of that mattered. I knew where I was going. At last open space gave way to a house. Houses. A small town. Monsieur Fournier had taken me to visit my sister.

Chapter 20

Edith looked fine. My *pleurnicheuse* had no complaints.
Madame Chaput kept a clean, inviting house. Monsieur
Chaput worked for the railroad. They had a boy near Edith's
age, a black Scottish terrier and, among other items, a radio.
They would have heard the newscasts about Lyon. Monsieur
and Madame didn't appear worried, though. I was shy with
adults but I must have said something. They assured me no
bombs had fallen on the city. Where, they wondered, was
Monsieur Fournier getting his information. I was confused.
Why would Monsieur Fournier repeat rumors picked up
at a café – terrible rumors, at that – without having them
confirmed? And what were his reasons for telling me?

Once Madame Fournier realized I knew how to find Edith's
house she let me go there on my own. I'd present myself
at the door asking, "Can Edith come for a walk?" Her first
question was always, "Did you hear from Maman and Papa?"

I would say, "No, did you?" No, no, no. This conversation
would make us both sad. I'd try to brighten the mood with
some of the funnier aspects of life with the Fourniers. I told
her of the impact my toothbrush made. And about the cow
and goat who woke me each morning from the other side of
my "bedroom" wall. That provoked a smile. Well, it was really
only Gentille, pounding away with her goat horns. Pêchette
was quiet unless she was anxious to be milked. Then she had
a surprisingly loud moo. For Edith's benefit I demonstrated

just how loud. And there were the table manners notable
for their absence. The noises that digestion produces and we
thought everyone learned to suppress were allowed natural
release with no need for apologies. I conveyed these facts
to my sister using more direct language. She roared with
laughter. Not having to say *pardon* tickled her most. We were
both thin but Edith hadn't lost weight. She seemed to be
doing better than I was. "I wash my underpants every night,"
she confided solemnly. I had taught her how so I inwardly
claimed my share of the credit.

I was glad the journey to Edith's and back took me through
a forest. Enveloped by woods, I was in a place out of time.
There – there were the high ferns. And mushrooms I hadn't
seen since I was very small, red with white dots. Poisonous
for sure, but pretty all the same. My friend Margaretchen and
I had searched for dwarves who made secret homes under
mushrooms like these. We were four years old. And here were
the strange bushes that looked like little trees.

Margaretchen and I used to stare awestruck at the great pines.
We thought they were alive. Not alive like a running brook or
plants that grow but alive like stately giants with outstretched
arms. We were never afraid of the giants or anything else
in our enchanted forestland. I felt a rush of freedom,
remembering and imagining. I was very young, walking with
Opa on the grounds of a fine old estate. Opa long ago, before
I renamed him *Grandpère*. He knew about birds and insects
and furry creatures that froze in their tracks and were then out
of sight in an instant. If only he had stayed with us. Not a day

went by that I didn't think of him. I could picture him here, right now, easygoing in his hat and jacket and walking stick, his hand waiting for mine. It seemed almost possible.

One day, during my second week, I scrambled down toward the brook intending to scoop pebbles. Marcel warned me, "Don't drink the water. The *gendarmes* are hunting for Jews in the forest. The brook is poisoned."

"The brook … poisoned! Why …?"

"To make them come out – so they can't survive in hiding."

My beautiful brook! I hoped it wasn't true. It hadn't been true about bombs falling on Lyon. Marcel wouldn't tell me if he didn't believe it himself. His concern for my safety was genuine. Monsieur Fournier probably believed the bomb story he brought home from the café, but I couldn't help feeling he took some poorly disguised pleasure in seeing me react. A trace of amusement hovered around his mouth. But Marcel was utterly straightforward and trustworthy. He wouldn't want to scare me. Maybe I wasn't included in the camaraderie of shepherds, but he never forgot I was with him on the meadow and that he was responsible for me.

I sat alone on the grass and tried not to think about the brook. My eyes kept returning to the water that flowed clear as before. *Lucky for brooks that they aren't people and can't know when they've been violated. Marcel said Jews were hiding in the forest. If they were hiding, what was I doing?* For the first time I confronted the true purpose of this no-holiday holiday. I lay back, my arm across my face shutting out the swift moving clouds and birds overhead, the distant mountains low against the sky. An idea disturbed my mind, pulled me upright in alarm. If police are searching the forest in this nowhere place, what can be happening to Maman and Papa?

Chapter 21

Bang! Another morning with Gentille pounding her side of the partition, accenting her message with occasional plaintive bleats. Groggy, holding close my portion of blanket, I rolled over. It made no difference. The noise issued from behind my head, the volume and vibration unchanged no matter where I was positioned. But other reasons prompted me to shift location. In my alcove bed – the bed big enough for three or four girls my size – were three more girls. I wondered what they thought about our rural-style wake-up. They'd been here a few days but I kept silent. They didn't talk to me so I didn't talk to them. They had come from St. Etienne and must have known each other. Whispering, giggling, they seemed to be having a good time. I assumed they were ordinary French girls in le Chambon for a vacation, maybe relatives of the Fourniers. They ignored me. At night I lay narrow, allowing for room between them and me. But in the morning I felt their breath in my hair. I wriggled away again to the thump of the goat's horns and the sound of her intermittent *eh-eh-ehs*. I was nearing the end of my second week at the farmhouse. The noise still startled me when I first opened my eyes, before I recognized the source. Then I found it oddly reassuring.

They tagged along, following Marcel and me and the animals to the fields. Marcel let us go down to the brook. I don't know if the danger had ever been real. The waters that ran from the mountains would quickly have washed away any poisons. The forest, too, was clear of invaders and I could cross the

151

brook and admire the ferns if I wanted. I hadn't forgotten that policemen had been there, hunting for people like … me. That part of the story I believed to be true. I stayed alone at the water's edge, collecting pebbles. The others invented their own games.

Excluded from the society of the new girls, I convinced myself I was a pariah. In my mind they were all Monique, Monique times three, from old, secure families. French families. And sly, knowing, they instantly perceived my difference. That I was only an almost French girl. A not Catholic, not Protestant, not any brand of Christian, almost French girl. Usually it had been all right being who I was. But not always. It wasn't all right with Madame de C., who said it wasn't all right with our great leader, Maréchal Pétain, and it definitely wasn't all right with the police in the forest.

I decided the girls weren't related to the Fourniers. Nobody acted familiar enough. Their parents were probably paying to give them a holiday in the country. A strange holiday but at least they weren't hiding. My sister was hiding, as I was. She just didn't realize it. I gave the subject some thought and wondered why – if there was all this room in my bed – didn't Edith and I stay together? Another unasked, unanswered question.

At home my parents had stood between me and the news I saw on *Les Actualitiés* or heard on the radio or absorbed when adults didn't know I was listening. My parents were a great buffer against the need to make sense of threatening information. Leaving interpretation to them, I never learned to really worry. But here, turned inward and relying on no one, I was getting better at it. Soon I would be an expert. Since the supposed bombing of Lyon I'd been concerned about Maman and Papa. Now I added myself and Edith to the endangered list. My neck and shoulder developed unsettling new habits. They would tingle and cramp. I'd have an urgent need to twist my neck – first to the right, then to the left – as if someone inside was making me do it. I couldn't control or stop it. Madame Fournier watched. When mealtimes came she urged me to accept extra food, her best attempt at a cure.

During the third week Monsieur Fournier drew me aside. "Don't expect to find your parents alive," he said. "Yesterday they picked up every remaining Jew in Lyon." If only half of what he was saying was true, my parents were in grave danger.

The next morning I stuffed all my things into my knapsack. I had so few belongings taking them raised no suspicions. I told Madame Fournier I was going to visit my sister. She nodded her assent. *Good. They won't miss me for a while.* I grabbed a hunk of bread from the table – breakfast – and walked through the bright green door for the last time, on to the grazing fields, down to the brook, across the bridge of stones and through the forest. I was calm. I knew what I had to do. As a side benefit, with each step I was increasing the distance between the clique and me. From the moment they moved in I had been afraid they might betray me.

Later I understood. My three non-companions were most likely Jewish, too, and as frightened of me as I was of them.

Chapter 22

What I told Madame Fournier was true: I was going to visit Edith.

Madame Chaput was surprised to find me at the door so early. "You and Edith are walking this morning?"

I shook my head. "We have to go home."

I must have said this with conviction. Madame Chaput didn't question me but assumed some qualified adult had made the decision. Monsier Chaput, the railroad man, helpfully advised us on when and where to catch the train. Edith and I set out with high expectations. Our family would be together again.

Buying tickets separated me from the rest of my money. No problem. Soon we would be with Maman and Papa. We chose a compartment and sat side by side, my arm around Edith. A grown-up eleven year-old and a not so grown-up nine year-old.

The trip wasn't direct. I remembered that from before. We got off the first train and waited for the loudspeaker to announce the track to Lyon. My plan was going smoothly. I didn't mind that the trains were local and slow. Getting home took about four hours, including the streetcar to Villeurbanne and the ten-block walk to our apartment on the *premier étage,* the first floor that is actually a second floor.

Trembling with excitement, I rang the bell. No answer. No

sound from behind the locked door. We waited and tried again. Nothing.

We walked down the stairs and back outside and crossed the street to the square where Renée and I used to run with our friends, and where Edith had introduced her variations on hopscotch to an unreceptive audience. But this was midsummer. The children were gone. The benches were empty. Edith and I settled on one that provided a clear view of the door to our apartment house. No one entering or leaving would escape our notice.

"Maybe they're shopping," I offered.

"Maybe," Edith echoed, uncertain. I hadn't let her in on all the possible reasons for anxiety.

The afternoon dragged toward evening. My parents didn't generally go walking this late. If my mother went out she didn't stay long. Papa would need her. A few people exited and entered the building, none of them resembling my parents. Papa was always easy to spot from afar with his cane, his gait, his proud bearing. Another hour, an hour and a half.

Edith said, "I'm hungry." I was too. I avoided meeting her eyes. I knew she was getting upset. Only now did it hit me, the enormity of what I'd done. Here we were, two children alone. We'd spent our money. For all we knew, Maman and Papa had vanished. I'd pulled my little sister from a safe hiding place and was now completely responsible for her. *Maybe Monsieur Fournier was right. Maybe they …!* I couldn't bring myself to finish the dreadful thought.

"Let's try again," I said. Clutching each other's hands, we headed back to the apartment. We forced ourselves to keep an ordinary pace. Running would have attracted attention. We climbed the single flight and maybe – with no one in the hall to watch - allowed ourselves a short burst of speed to our door. A gentle, familiar voice spoke.

"Renée, Renée Kann …" The blind man, Maman's masseur in the next apartment, had recognized my step or guessed my identity from the desperate knocking and jiggling he heard.

"*C'est vous?*" Is that you?

"*Oui!*"

"*Vous cherchez vos parents?*" You are looking for your parents?

"*Oui!*"

"*Ils sont chez le concierge du Théâtre Municipal.*"

With the concierge of the Municipal Theater – that could only be Renée's father!

"*Merci, merci, Monsieur!*" I grabbed Edith's hand and we were off. My worst fears were over. My parents were close by. Yet I would never have thought to go there. Renée was the one link between her parents and mine and she was away for the whole summer.

"Renée!" Madame Caussidière's voice was almost a whisper. Her eyes darted through the hall as if checking for observers. "You can't come in." It wasn't the welcome I expected. "Go sit in the square. I will send your *maman*."

Madame Caussidière kept her word. Maman was aghast to find us. She took us back to our apartment, then returned to the Caussidières to get food for our supper. She divided the evening between us and Papa, who remained with his hosts. I told Maman why I left the Fourniers and couldn't go back. She had no idea how miserable I'd been. She didn't rebuke me for putting myself and Edith in danger or even for running off without permission. I'd been a rule-following, may-I-be-excused kind of girl. If I needed to get away that badly there had to be a reason. She didn't take long to understand that I did it for them, for her and Papa, because of the stories that made me worry. My explanations were punctuated by sudden jerking of my neck and shoulders, convincing her, if she required convincing, of the fear I had endured.

Obviously, Edith and I wanted to know how our parents got stationed beneath the Municipal Theater in the one-room ground floor apartment of the Caussidières. Maman told us some of it.

Renée's father had heard rumors of a major action to be taken against Jews still living in the *quartier*, the neighborhood. Though the Caussidières had never met my parents they knew where we lived. Renée probably told them. She must have said we were Jewish, or they figured it out, helped along, perhaps, by her remarks about the taste of our Passover matzo. I couldn't picture my friend and her parents talking easily, the way we did in my family. But I guess it happened. Maybe sharing a meal brought on communication, bridged the generation gap. Even the Caussidières had to exchange a few words while they ate. But Renée had been out of town for weeks. Only strong conscience would have compelled her parents to step forward.

Maman didn't want to alarm us with every detail. She didn't tell us that the entire Municipal Building had been taken over by the Pétain police, whose sole purpose was to enforce the laws against the Jews. Monsieur Caussidière hadn't far to go to pick up the rumors. The public bathroom offered outstanding opportunities for eavesdropping. Since the family lacked a bathroom of their own, Monsieur Caussidière often found himself among Vichy henchmen in relaxed mode, casually conversing, discussing their plans. In this case an imminent event, a *rafle*. They didn't censor their comments in the presence of the man with the keys. To them, a custodian was a person of no account. Besides underestimating what it takes to keep a complicated building working, they underestimated this custodian.

Renée's father lost no time in knocking at our door, introducing himself to Papa, explaining why they must follow him at once. Renée's mother prepared the big screened-off bed. The Caussidières slept on Renée's bed and a chair.

The next night, the two couples were roused very late by a commotion outdoors. Trucks waited with their lights beaming, illuminating the square. A disheveled crowd was being assembled. Sleepers had been awakened in their beds, rushed out of their apartments, flashlights shining in their faces. My parents and Renée's watched from the safety of the darkened room as neighbors were marched onto the trucks. Maman recognized some of her friends.

My mother was wise to spare us this information. Excited by our adventure, relieved by a reunion that almost wasn't, Edith and I didn't need an overload of truth. Maman settled us in our beds. "You are both big girls," she said, "taking trains on your own. I have to go to Papa now. You'll be fine and I'll be back in the morning."

The night felt short, not very peaceful. Maman must consider us grown-up, we thought, impressed to be sleeping unsupervised for the first time.

We rose early and gathered our things. My mother shepherded us through the city, back to the tangled, cobblestone streets that led to the office of Madame Dreyfus. Before we could say Le Chambon-sur-Lignon we were sitting across from her on a train, heading back to the plateau, a farming region where there were no ski resorts and the people had little because the soil wasn't rich. But Le Chambon possessed its own austere beauty and in 1942 it was, for us, the safest spot in France. Madame Dreyfus, employing the most delicate tact, forgot to mention our escapade. Maybe she understood a little of what propelled me to abandon the Fourniers.

Edith and I hadn't seen our father at all. We knew Maman would do anything to protect his nerves, like not telling him we were in town and why we had fled back home.

Chapter 23

Edith returned to the Chaputs. For me, Madame Dreyfus came through with a major improvement. I was placed in a boardinghouse, the Pension Royer, run by two young women. Mesdemoiselles Royer. They were sisters. Six to eight girls around my age were staying with them in a large house built of stone. It was set on a generous-sized property near Les Tavas, one of the tiny villages that surround Le Chambon. We were close to the main road so I never felt isolated. I was introduced as a niece. Soon I discovered that the other girls were supposed to be nieces too. And girls arriving after me were also presented to the group as nieces. Which ones actually were – if any – I didn't know.

Some of us shared a room. There were four girls in mine, including me. Unlike the last place, we had individual beds. All the girls in the *pension* ate together and took long walks trying to find flowers or looking for berries that were safe to eat. The elderberries tasted delicious, but you had to remember to stop after the first several if you didn't want a horrible upset stomach. The first time I tried them, I forgot and ate too many. I wasn't the only one. It didn't happen again.

We took turns washing, drying and putting away dishes. We picked vegetables, cleaned and sliced them in the large kitchen. We did our own laundry, laying it out on the grass to dry.

There was a shelf of children's books. Some appealed to girls our age. For thrills you could do worse than the Jules Verne adventures that promised breathtaking voyages to the center of the earth or thousands of leagues beneath the sea. Or you could sink into a weepy tale called *Sans Famille*, by Hector Malot, about a boy who escaped from an orphanage only to find life on the outside not much better. Rejected by everyone, he managed to grow up anyway. *François le Champi*, by Georges Sand, also featured an abandoned child, this one discovered in the fields as an infant. Georges Sand wrote other popular children's books like *La Petite Fadette* and *La Mare au Diable* (The Devil's Pond).

France hadn't yet produced a vast body of children's literature. The same titles tended to appear and reappear in every collection. It was no surprise to find my old friends, *Les Malheurs de Sophie* and *Les Petites Filles Modèles*. Chances were, if it was a book for my age I had read it before, more than once if it was good. But that didn't dampen my eagerness to hold it again and begin on page one. I waited patiently for my favorites to make the rounds and return to me.

The Royers read newspapers. None of the girls were interested. Stories about what was happening in the world scared us.

I never knew what the other children thought of me and I didn't discuss any of them. I didn't pick a special girl to confide in. We were friendly but not friends. At least there were no cliques. That was a relief.

The long-established residents of Le Chambon, generations

161

of families, didn't allow themselves excess words. We who had recently joined them quickly absorbed the habit of guarding our tongues. I already had practice being quiet about some things. I started learning two years ago when I lost my membership in Les Guides. "Don't say much when you meet people," Madame Dreyfus had warned. "Don't discuss your religion. No need to tell them where you are from." The Royer sisters made her advice easy to follow. Being introduced as a niece set the tone.

All the same, there was nothing solemn about the atmosphere. The two ladies knew that regular hours, short, light conversations, outdoor exercise, good food, books to read and the expectation to help with chores would convince "their" girls that life away from home could be normal. They never behaved as though having us with them was the least bit of trouble. I stopped considering myself a pariah. The muscles in my neck and shoulder took the cue. My tic would last a few more months, but at so mild a level people had to tell me I was doing it, or else I wouldn't know.

Sometimes word filtered through that the police would be paying a visit. Then the Royer sisters sent us on "errands" in the fields, along a small rivulet. They didn't explain why we had to vacate the house or for how long. The errands – like picking berries – didn't seem urgent. But the suddenness of the assignment, the no-argument tone of voice, told us to stay away until we got an all-clear message.

These efforts didn't always work. Two men in plain clothes were standing in the dining room as we sat down for a noon meal. We sensed immediately they were policemen. One of them murmured something to the younger Mademoiselle Royer. "My nieces," she said, smiling.

The man said, *"Bien."* Very well. He wasn't smiling. The older Mademoiselle Royer ladled out the soup. It was cream of leek. Edith and I never ate creamed soups. Maman never served them. Creamed soups could interfere with eating a main course that included meat, which it often did. The dietary laws forbid the mixing of milk and meat or even eating one close in time to the other. By now I had developed a revulsion that extended to every creamed soup – the whole category, but especially cream of leek because I knew Papa hated leeks. The prospect of swallowing the thick greenish liquid and its submerged chunks of vegetable – the very thought – struck down my appetite.

I stared at the bowl. The other girls apparently had no problem with cream of leek soup. The second plainclothesman leaned against the doorway, casting an impassive eye on the little "nieces." If I didn't eat, he would know at once I was of the people who refuse to mix milk and meat. To me it wasn't far-fetched. I seriously imagined that the authorities in this remote locale had mastered the subtle markers of a Jewish upbringing. And if not – if his curiosity glided past my resistance to the *soupe du jour* – it might settle on the question of how I was related to my "aunts" or the other nieces! We should be cousins. What if I knew nothing about my "cousins"? I didn't realize that this was the more probable danger. But I knew I must at all costs avoid

163

becoming the center of attention.

I dipped my spoon, raised it to my lips, gulped and did it again, until the bowl was empty. The officials withdrew. I rushed from the table, sure that my face had turned a pale green, the color of the soup. If the nieces – or whoever they were – noticed, I hoped they wouldn't make anything of it.

◊ ◊ ◊

Edith visited me if she could, especially if she was sad or wanted me to steer her out of some quandary. She stood at the door one day in obvious distress.

"What's wrong?" I wanted to know. Pale and silent, she presented her hand. *"Mon Dieu!* How did that happen? Did you show Madame Chaput?"

"I can't."

"What do you mean you can't?"

"Because she told me not to play with him."

"With who, her son?"

"No!"

Despite her pain Edith was laughing. The Chaputs had warned her about playing with their little black Scottie. (I'd forgotten about the dog.) *"Il a mauvais caractère,"* they said. He's not reliable. He gets into bad moods. However, Edith and the terrier would allow nothing to hinder their developing fellowship.

"Today he was really friendly, sniffing me," she said, confident I would understand. The sniffing led to light hand-nibbling. The nibbling raised cautions. She pulled back too suddenly. He snapped, biting through the nail of her middle finger.

I considered activating my trusty Croix Rouge kit. Hadn't Maman packed it for just such a purpose? It contained gauze, tape, scissors and a bottle of iodine. I thought again. An adult had better see this. I'd already risked disaster hauling Edith to Villeurbanne. That time we were lucky. I decided we would consult the younger Mademoiselle Royer.

She cleaned the wound with hydrogen peroxide and helped while I did the bandaging. Edith was stoic through it all, something I should have expected. But on each occasion when fortitude was demanded she quietly astonished me.

Walking with her to the Chaputs I asked, "How will you explain that?" pointing to the wrapped finger. She furrowed her brow, then fixed on a satisfactory solution.

"If I don't tell, they won't ask." Edith lost the nail but no infection set in. I never did learn whether Madame Chaput found out.

August became September. Along the brook the elderberries ripened to deep purple. The leaves of wild witch hazel, with their raised reddish yellow speckles, were changing to a duller green. The plateau had never been hot, not even in high summer, and it was always cool when the sun slipped behind the mountains. We reached late September. The night air was chillier but I barely registered the difference. Girls had come and gone since I arrived. The group around me was thinning. Just when it seemed I would stay forever one of the ladies beckoned to me. Madame Dreyfus had telephoned.

I brought Edith back to spend the last few days at the *pension*. We had to be ready to leave together. On the morning of our departure the other girls were out. I couldn't say *au revoir* to them. Mesdemoiselles Royer, older and younger – though both fairly young, hugged us, navigating round the knapsacks on our shoulders. They spoke briefly with Madame Dreyfus. Then we were on our way. This time Maman and Papa were expecting us.

Riding the trains to Lyon, I looked ahead to the school year. I wasn't going to miss the first day, when the *lycée* opened. A whole new experience awaited me, far from the scene of my last day at the Ecole Anatole France. I pushed aside the image of Madame de C. holding the book, holding me up to public humiliation. Even knowing that Renée Caussidière would still be attending failed to reawaken affection for my old elementary school. Anyway, Renée was returning from – now I remembered – Marseilles, where her grandparents, aunts and uncles lived. And cousins, real cousins. We would compare holidays.

I would tell her about a farmhouse on a high plateau so distant and quiet it seemed at the end of the world. A cow and a goat had their stable on the other side of the wall where my bed was. And Gentille thumped the partition behind my head early in the morning and bleated like my own alarm clock. I'd tell her how Marcel led the animals to the meadow and I came along to watch the sky and collect pebbles at the brook. That was when I noticed the ferns across the water, near the forest, and discovered I could travel on the bridge of stones. Marcel and his mother were kind but the father frightened me and knew he was doing it. None of them had seen a toothbrush. They had one towel and used it for drying everything from feet to dishes to cheese. Then the three girls came. They shut me out. I didn't trust them. I got so worried, especially about my parents, I had to take Edith and run away.

Renée would be surprised I did that. I'd tell her about the *pension*, how much better it was, but still unusual, with all of us supposed to be nieces. She wouldn't believe how brave Edith had been getting bandaged from the dog bite. She had Edith pegged for a *pleurnicheuse* through and through. Finally I would describe my encounter with the cream of leek soup and the two men in plain clothes, an episode most unfunny to me. But I could see Renée finding the humor. She'd say something like, "Well, that's one way to get spoiled brats eating what's put in front of them!"

Chapter 24

Edith and I joined our parents in the apartment, as I had
expected. But we weren't alone. Monsieur and Madame Lion,
recently arrived from the Occupied Zone, had moved in.
They were longtime friends from the Sarreguemines days.
When they couldn't find a place in the Lyon area it was
natural for Maman and Papa to make room for them. Their
son, the famous Henri, was lodging with Tante Grit and her
family. Georges, Henri's older brother, had been arrested and
deported earlier that year.

Discovering that we had visitors wasn't a shock. We'd taken in
refugees before - friends and friends of friends - and complete
strangers. This was different. The Lions were here to stay. Not
with us but with our apartment, furniture and all. We were the
ones who must prepare to leave.

"Is Renée at home?" I asked my mother.

"I don't think so."

"I'll go see …" I said.

"No," said Maman, almost before I could get the words out.
"Let's not bother the Caussidières. When Renée returns she's
sure to come here."

I shrugged, puzzled at the refusal. I'd tapped on Renée's
window a thousand times. Maman, of course, hadn't told

us about the *Milice,* and how they were using the Municipal Building as their headquarters.

Our comings and goings were kept to a minimum. Opening the door, never automatic, was handled with great caution. When we heard a knock we went silent until a voice identified itself. We had an arrangement with the concierge, a woman whose apartment was on our floor, at the top of the stairs facing all comers. Anyone entering or leaving the building would have to deal with her. At the very least he wouldn't pass unobserved. She had assured my parents that she knew how to delay an interloper, send him in the wrong direction and, if need arose, get us out of our rooms into hers. The apartments had back doors that opened to a common mezzanine. The Lions knew that after we left, they could depend on her.

During the short time that remained to us in Villeurbanne, my parents engaged in a curious activity. According to the papers they'd recently acquired, they had ceased to be Edmond and Friedel Kann and had become Louis Pierre Weber and Marie Cécile Catherine Weber. That was a lot of names. They questioned each other endlessly, practicing their new identities. Edith and I were allowed to keep our first names but we had to get used to being Webers if we wanted to match our parents. I managed a convincing transition but Edith, when asked for her name, replied in a thin uncertain voice. Coached away from her hesitancy she sounded stiff and rehearsed. We were worried.

Maman said, "Edith, you're wearing your new name like a pair

169

of new shoes. You've got to make it sound like a pair of old shoes, as though you've been Edith Weber forever."

Edith digested Maman's proposal. She said, "Hmm," and proceeded to shuffle around the room, her feet encased in an invisible pair of beat-up slippers. Striving to make the unfamiliar familiar, she recited, "Edith Weber, Edith Weber, Edith Weber, Edith …"

"That's right," I encouraged. "Now imagine it's as easy as jumping into the swimming pool …"

"Edith Weber, Edith Weber, splash, splash, Edith Weber… splash…!"

"Now you're sooo natural! Like a cat says meow, a duck says quack … a cow says moo … and Edith says WEBER!"

"Edith Weber, Weber, Weber, quack, moo, meow!"

"Okay. What's your name?"

"Edith Weber."

Good. She could have fooled me. Rattling off a false name isn't simple, especially if you normally tell the truth. I was hoping that this was a skill my sister wouldn't have to demonstrate. I was hoping the same for myself. Maman and Papa didn't take their own abilities for granted. Over and over went the questions and answers.

"Madame," Papa intoned, playing the part of the pompous official, "please tell me your entire name."

"Marie Cécile Catherine Weber."

"And what was your maiden name?"

"Muller."

"And the first names of your parents?"

"Pierre and Jeanne."

"Ah," said Papa, as if to trip her up, "but what is your mother's maiden name?"

Maman was not to be confounded. "Lorsong. She was born Jeanne Lorsong." So there.

Sometimes the make-believe bordered on nonsense, or crossed the line. Papa continued.

"It says you are from Lorraine."

"*Oui.*" He pretended to stamp a document.

"And what is the purpose of your travels?"

"To visit friends, Monsieur. But already I miss the society of my animals. My cows and my pigs." She dabbed an imaginary tear.

"How touching to encounter a woman who is French to the core, with such profound connections to the land!"

"And to the beasts," Maman added piously. "French beasts. Creatures of the good Lord."

The bizarre dialogue had nowhere to go. Until the next wave of inspiration, my parents rested their talents.

We didn't mind going through memory exercises with the Lions around. But if Maman and Papa were to discuss anything top secret, they waited for privacy. They wanted at least Monsieur Lion out of earshot. He was known to forget himself and talk too much. Unlike the people of Le Chambon, unlike many of us by now, he had insufficiently established the habit of guarding his tongue.

While the Lions were living in Blois, a city in the Occupied Zone, police had entered their home in search of their older boy, Georges. Instead of saying, "He's gone away, we don't know where," instead of keeping quiet, this father who loved his son volunteered, "He'll be back soon!" The police waited outside and arrested Georges as he walked down the busy street to his door.

This happened during the past school year when I was in grade five. I remembered how I tried not to believe it – Georges was only sixteen. Months had gone by with no word from him. I saw his parents every day but managed not to think about how they must feel, knowing that a little caution, a little silence, could have saved their son.

Madame Lion was the second wife of Monsieur Lion. His first wife, Georges' mother, had died. (Henri was the child of both parents in the new marriage.) But Madame Lion didn't grieve any less. She loved Georges as if he were her own.

We began to pack two suitcases. We could only take what we absolutely needed and nothing else. Any object that displayed our original names, our true addresses, had to be left behind. That meant stories and drawings I had done for school, books with my name inscribed, letters and artwork from Opa. I tried to salvage this or that, saying, "Maybe just …"

Maman shook her head. "We cannot take a chance." Later, confronted with the pile of books and papers I'd reluctantly surrendered, she said, "Choose what matters most. The Lions will keep a few things for you."

I thought of Tante Grit, Oncle Simon and the boys "What about them?" I asked. "Are they staying in their apartment?"

"No," said Maman, "they're going south to the Midi."

"Why are the Lions staying, but not us or the Epsteins?"

"Our last names, Kann and Epstein, tell the world we're probably foreign and Jewish. Lion can be a French name."

As we got closer to leaving, Edith and I stepped up our practice sessions. We needed to know not only our new last names but our supposed Lorraine address and our parents' many names. There were limits to how long we could keep at it with straight faces.

"And what is your mother's name, Mademoiselle?" I, the stern bureaucrat, asked for the umpteenth time. Edith gazed vacantly at the ceiling.

"My mother's name is…Maman."

"Come now, young lady, every mother's name is Maman."

"Ma-ma-ma." Edith strummed her lower lip.

The real Maman suggested, "Why don't we say Edith is large for her age? She's actually two years old!"

"I'm two years old. One, two," said Edith, holding up her fingers.

"Why two, why not six months?" I said, topping one tall tale with another.

"Ga-ga-goo …"

Someone rapped at the door. We froze.

"*C'est moi* – open up."

We relaxed at the familiar voice of Maman's masseur. He had come to say *au revoir*. Maman guided him through the door over to the sofa, but he protested. "I am here only *un moment*."

Maman said, "You have met the Lions?" Yes, they had met. He wanted them to understand he was another line of defense, like the concierge.

"Anything different on our floor – I know it right away," he said, touching his ear. "Any trouble – you can come to me. Don't wait because that can make the difference."

"Thank you again, Monsieur, for helping me and Edith," I was surprised to hear myself say without being asked.

"Is that Mademoiselle Renée? Well, you are most welcome, you and Edith. I am so glad I was in that afternoon."

October 1, 1942, dawned cool and overcast. Maman and I carried out the suitcases. I'd been home less than a week. In the gray light I looked one last time at the square – at the fountain, its basin dry, at the empty concrete benches and the trees and bushes where we used to take cover for hide-and-seek. I looked across to the Caussidières' window. When Renée got back I would be gone. In another week the *lycée* would open without me.

"I really wanted to start my new high school," I said to Papa.

"There's always another *lycée*," he retorted. He noticed my dejection. Usually I kept disappointments to myself.

"We're off on a … new adventure," he said. "And you're my best adventurer, the best traveler in the family. My red-haired Gypsy." He placed his good hand lightly on my head.

Papa hadn't told me the *lycée* I'd hoped to enter wasn't accepting Jewish students anymore. As for Renée Caussidière, I never saw her again.

Chapter 25

Only Papa had actually met the *passeur*. That was when they negotiated the particulars of our trip and the cost of his services. The *passeur* didn't sell his expertise at a cut rate. Nor was the wish to help people a primary motive, if it figured at all. Papa had to agree to part with a heavy chunk of his lifetime savings. Obviously, Edith and I weren't told any of the financial details or let in on the nature of the deal: illegal and secret. For our benefit, a *passeur* was a gentleman who had consented to be our guide.

My father's gaze roamed the platform of the Lyon-Brotteau railroad station. Where was he, our smuggler of human beings? Papa caught sight of him. They connected briefly, and then the man turned his glance away. He had looked toward us long enough for me to notice an oddness to his face, something about the focus of his eyes. I couldn't tell the cause.

When it was time to board, he chose a bench at a far remove from ours. We were well into the journey, our train making its predictable stops. At the Aix-les-Bains station it sat idle longer than usual. Maybe the officials were going to check everybody's identity papers, a disturbing possibility. The *passeur* must have been of this opinion, because he disembarked, leaving us on our own. When he decided that the period of uncertainty had ended, he reappeared and took his safely-away-from-us seat. The train rolled forward.

"Where are we going?" asked Edith.

Maman showed us the tickets. They read: Lyon-Annecy-Geneva-Basel. Geneva and Basel were in Switzerland. That was where we were going. No one had told me, but I knew. What was all the memorizing for? The memorizing and the playacting. And I was sure we wouldn't be on this train all the way into the new country. That would be too simple.

Without speaking, Maman pointed to one of the names on the ticket. I'd learned about it in school from geography lessons. I remembered how it looked on a map, very close to the border with Switzerland, just south of Lac Léman. Annecy, the next major stop. The last stop in France.

We got off before we reached the city in order to avoid guards and checkpoints and questions. The *passeur* led us to a restaurant where we had lunch. I can't say what we ate except that it was good. The people who worked there seemed to know him. He must have been a regular, along with the travelers he brought. The waiters, the owner – they clearly understood what he was up to and where we were headed. Sitting at the table, I observed his face at close range. I was right. There was something peculiar. One eye was shiny and didn't move with the other. I don't think I realized it was glass.

After the meal we prepared to take the bus into Annecy. It was a small bus called an *autocar*. The time was around two o'clock.

"Disappear right away when you get off," he whispered as we boarded. "Leave your suitcases on the ground. I'll bring them later."

The final stop was at a railroad station. We climbed down, dropped our suitcases and walked without looking back – not too fast, not too slow. No one interfered. Our designated meeting spot was another restaurant.

My parents ordered coffee for themselves and lemonade for me and Edith. *Limonade*. It came in a bottle. We tried to be patient, waiting for the guide and the suitcases. This was a crucial juncture in our expedition. It was widely known that people were trying to cross over to Switzerland from Annecy. The French police were on the lookout. Anyone caught attempting to breach the border would be arrested and sent to a camp, and from there deported to Germany and beyond. My parents were completely aware of this. Edith and I knew nothing, but we sensed the gravity of our circumstances. Our mysterious guide's efforts to pretend we were strangers weren't lost on us. And why did we have to wait and wait? And what was our true destination and why the stops and detours? I noticed that my parents were breathing quickly. Nerves spread fast. Soon we were all taking tight, shallow breaths, as if the air itself might fail us.

Suddenly, there he was, carrying the two suitcases. Although it had seemed like an eternity, we'd only waited half an hour. With a few strides he reached our table.

"Stay in this place," said the *passeur*, fixing his one living eye on Papa. "Someone will come before dark."

It had been hours. This time really hours. We moved with our baggage to a small room at the back of the restaurant. Outside, daylight had softened to dusk.

Papa bought more lemonade for Edith and me. It gave us something to do, though we weren't thirsty. We reminded ourselves a long wait was part of the plan. That should have made us feel better than it did. I thought we could play a word game.

"Maman," I began, but she wasn't interested. She looked frightened, her mind turned inward. I had never seen her like this.

The door of the restaurant opened. A man with a club-foot limped toward us. Our next link. The expression on his face didn't make me want to trust him. If anything, he projected a quality that encouraged suspicion. He had already removed his hat. His dark hair was plastered down with some kind of grease. A beret protruded from his jacket pocket. Compared to this one, our first *passeur* – even considering his shifty maneuvers – had been positively comforting.

The man nodded hello and dropped a bit of news. Did we know that forty-five people were arrested at the border yesterday and sent to deportation camps? No, we did not. Dragging his unwieldy leg, he moved to the side and signaled for Papa to join him. They had private matters to discuss. With the danger so high, our need so urgent, maybe he was going to ask for more money.

But the information had another effect. My mother turned
pale and started to shiver. Maman! I pressed close to her.
Edith hugged her from the other side. Maman was our rock.
This couldn't be happening. I left the table and went to where
Papa and the man were talking. Disagreeing was more like it.
I asked Papa for his handkerchief. He looked over at Maman
and Edith and understood something was wrong.

I took the handkerchief to a sink behind the bar, held it
under the cold running water, squeezed it out and folded
it. I returned to Maman and laid the compress against her
forehead. I felt the shivering subside. Edith had her arm
around Maman and was stroking her hand. Papa didn't
intervene. He could see we had things under control. And
Maman did grow calmer. The panic lifted. Gradually, she
recovered herself.

Papa and the man suspended their discussion, though it was
clear they hadn't reached an accord. It was fully dark when,
to our surprise and relief, the first guide returned. We were on
track again, no longer at the sole mercy of the vaguely sinister
man with the clubfoot. Soon, though, the two *passeurs* were
combining their energies as they negotiated with my father for
the final payment.

Together they haggled for more money. They repeated the
story of yesterday's arrests, trying to jack the fee higher.
Papa resisted.

"We have an agreement," he countered. Papa could be stubborn when he believed he was right. Besides, he had no more francs to give. A man could not travel penniless with a wife and children. Unexpectedly, the *passeurs* gave up their tactics and accepted the money they were offered. Maybe they realized the sort of group photo they would have made – one man with a glass eye, another with a clubfoot, the third frozen on one side from ancient war injuries. In the end they probably sympathized with my father. Like them, he faced life with a handicap, asking no privileges. They were three men with something in common.

It was nearly eight o'clock when the first *passeur* departed. We wouldn't be seeing him again. The second man led us to a car on a side street. Neither the driver – disheveled – nor the automobile – old and ill-used – inspired our confidence. Having no other options, we got in. Amazingly, the car took off. The driver succeeded in coaxing it up some steep hills despite its difficulties and the distressed noises it produced, like a frail creature unjustly burdened. We were sure it would conk out at any moment, but it persisted until slowing to a stop in front of a French customs house. A customs house! No one had warned us.

Our *passeur* said, "Give me a minute ..." and lumbered out. We heard him tell the guard that we were residents of a nearby village. So much for the province of Lorraine and our memorized answers and our papers contradicting his statement. The guard beamed a flashlight in our faces.

"Allez," he said. What a relief. Better than the good cowboys riding over the hill. Better than the William Tell Overture.

We were still in France. Patrols roamed the border, and we never knew when we might be stopped. The car came to a halt and the man with the clubfoot got out. He would now be replaced by a much younger man wheeling a bicycle who emerged from nowhere, from a shadow. He set his bike on the car's running board, tied it with twine to the door handles, and slid in from the driver's side.

It was getting late. We rode until we reached what seemed to be a farm.

"Everybody out," he said, meaning everybody except the driver, who pulled away.

We stepped carefully in the inky dark, tried to avoid creating noise. To see ahead we depended on the limited range of our young guide's flashlight. We entered a doorway and found ourselves in a barn, then passed through to a second door that opened out to the opposite side of the building, the side facing Switzerland. Along a far horizon were three small lights, like unblinking stars. Above us spread a black sky with no stars, no moon. I moved my hand in front of my face and saw nothing.

"You go to the middle light," said the young man, our third and final *passeur.* "They know you are coming. Go straight through the fields. Over on the right are trees. Stay clear of them. Patrols might be hiding."

The tone of his instructions alerted Papa. "We'll be following you, *oui?*" Silence. My parents had been allowed to believe that someone would accompany us all the way.

"I cannot," said the young man. No one spoke above a hush. Police could be anywhere, like in that cluster of trees to the right that we couldn't see.

The young man tried to buoy our spirits. "You can make it. The night is dark."

"Please," said Maman, "don't do this to us." But she appealed in vain. Our one remaining guide was leaving.

Chapter 26

We arranged ourselves in pairs. First Maman and me, with
Maman to my right. She had both suitcases and I shared
the weight on one side, my fingers touching hers as we
grasped the handle. To the right of Maman were Edith and
Papa with his cane. Edith had her arm under his free arm
and was holding his hand. Moving forward, we realized we
were stepping into freshly plowed fields, the parcels of land
separated by irrigation ditches.

It must have rained for a week. Mud clung to our shoes and
water seeped in, wetting our feet. The mud and water weighed
us down. We had no idea how much soggy, uneven acreage
stretched between us and the row of lights on the horizon.
The air carried an odor – not too pleasant but recognizable.
Leeks. The crop had just been harvested. The leftovers,
crushed, plowed under, were beginning to rot.

We made slow, damp progress. It was hard to calculate the
passing time and we didn't try. We concentrated on not
falling. If we forgot to keep looking ahead we would lose
our bearings and find only blackness in front of us. Then we
would have to stop and reorient ourselves toward the lights.

Something tugged at my arm. A small hand. Edith! She spoke
in a whisper. *"Papa est tombé!"* Papa has fallen.

He was lying down and couldn't get up, she said. His cane
was stuck in the mud. She took my hand and I followed with

Maman. We went to the right – we knew that much, and not too far right where the invisible trees clustered. Our eyes had become accustomed to the dark and we dimly perceived shadowy forms. We considered each one in hopes it could turn out to be Papa.

Somehow we discovered him, almost stumbled on him. He had managed to sit up. We helped him the rest of the way. With his useful arm he pried the cane from the sodden earth and asked Edith to carry it. He leaned on one of us for support as we made our way forward. Edith had kept a cool head. When she knew she couldn't lift Papa, couldn't call for help, and couldn't stay there, she did the one thing necessary to save our family. She found Maman and me.

As for Papa, he had been terrified for her once it came to him that they weren't together. What if she were lost? Now no one dared contemplate the what-ifs. We held each other close to regain our calm. If tight hugs could prevent future misadventures we were safe. I didn't think of it then, but Papa must have hated it doubly, being on the ground, immobile and muddy, in a field that smelled of leeks.

We trained our eyes toward the three lights. They didn't seem to be getting nearer even as we traveled toward them. But we knew they were real, not mirages in a desert. Added to the weight of clinging mud was the heaviness of fatigue. At least we were accounted for.

The middle light called us forward. When we got confused we'd find it again, our destination, our reminder that success was possible. Until we couldn't rely on it at all. As we advanced, new lights appeared to the left, and more to the right, and others in among them. An endless horizon of lights. Our steady beacon was lost among the multitude, and soon it was impossible to single it out. We shouldn't have worried. The changeable lights eventually provided their own remedy. One by one they went out, leaving a single illuminated window.

We approached a courtyard. A dog began to bark. A woman appeared and opened the gate. She said, "Come in and eat something." We followed her.

They'd been threshing grain the whole day, she explained, and had decided to stay up late to finish the job. We entered the large kitchen where she got a look at us – frightened, exhausted, our feet, legs, clothing caked and spattered with mud. Papa's suit was covered.

My mother asked, "Are we on Swiss soil?"

"Yes." This was so – literally – since we were inside. The farmhouse was in Switzerland while the front grounds were in France. The woman fed us hot soup, coffee, bread and jam.

"You're lucky," she said. "The border patrol left ten minutes ago."

Part Three

Hey, Red!

1942 – 1945

Summer 1939 – Diemeringen   February 1939 Sarreguemines

Summer 1941, st the parc of La Tête d'Or, Lyon

Chapter 27

The dark green waters of the Rhine that cut through the city of Basel flow beneath two bridges. If you're on one you can see the other. Between the bridges, high on a cliff called the Pfalz, rises the Muenster. Once it was a place of Catholic worship, and echoes, in every stone, its medieval origins. After the Reformation it became a Protestant cathedral.

From a terrace behind the church a long staircase descends to a simple building far below, perched on the river on stilts. You can enter it in your street clothes, pay a small admission fee and find the right changing room. You put on your bathing suit, get out on the deck, and ease or jump into the water. Near the deck is a roped-off area that's not as deep, the currents not as powerful as in the middle of the river. But this is no playpen. You'd better know what you're doing anywhere in the Rhine.

I make my way into the open water. If I wanted limits I'd stick to a swimming pool. I do the breaststroke. It's what I was taught. After a while I switch to a sort of sidestroke I have improvised for myself. I can relax and notice the feel and temperature and pull of the water. Walter Fischer swims beside me. He does a perfect crawl. I could never put it together, the synchronizing of arms, legs and breath. Walter is a strong swimmer. He's my friend – the closest thing I've had to a boyfriend – and river-swimming companion. No one dares come here alone. It is much too dangerous. You need buddies with you.

Walter will start ninth grade in September and I'll be in eighth. We attend different schools. He's at the *Realschule* and I'm at the *Maedchengymnasium*. It's early in the summer of 1944. I'm self-conscious in my one-piece bathing suit. When it's wet it clings. I'm no longer so thin, and my new figure makes me feel ungainly and ill-at-ease. Walter wears a pair of trunks and has no problem with his developing physique. I have a crush on him which I mustn't let him see. My friend Edith (not my sister) thinks he likes me too. I've decided he is the image of the god Apollo – an idea I picked up from the Greek mythology we studied last year. When I told Edith this she looked baffled. She is unfamiliar with Apollo. It doesn't matter. Edith has a crush on Heinz Weiss, not my type at all.

I glide to the middle of the river, to where I can see the two spires of the Muenster, my favorite sight. There they are, pointing skyward from behind a chestnut tree-covered terrace. Walter and I are moving toward the Wettsteinbruecke, the newer bridge, made of metal. Suddenly we are underneath. The water turns a shade darker and cold. Over our heads, the roar of cars and trams, the clangy bridge vibrations, shut out other sounds.

Swimming is becoming an effort. The water presses against us. We have to avoid the piers, the bridge's steel and concrete monster legs, where eddies spiral and currents meet and crash. I would never try this without Walter. We concentrate and manage to pass safely. Afterwards, coming back, we swim with the current. This would be easy except for where the current leads. I feel myself getting pulled toward one of the whirlpools swirling around the pier. If I don't break free I can be sucked deep into the river.

Walter speeds to my rescue, begins the work of towing me to a calmer location. His arm is around me. His hand grasps my waist, a hoped-for closeness that I'm too scared to appreciate.

I live on the other side of the river. Maman, Papa, Edith and I share a small apartment in an old house. All the houses are old. Most of the buildings in this neighborhood date from the seventeenth century. The area near the Muenster is old too – even older – but that part of the city has been carefully restored and maintained. It's called Gross Basel (Big Basel). Our section, Klein Basel (Little Basel), seems to have been neglected for hundreds of years. Where we live, the doorways are so low that anyone much taller than I has to duck. I guess people used to be shorter. The bathroom down the hall is like an indoor outhouse, with a toilet that doesn't flush. By some method, someone empties it. But we do have electricity and cold running water.

A Swiss couple and their curly-haired three-year-old live below us. Too often I see little Denise alone in a corridor. Her parents are fighting again. She closes her eyes and faces the wall, as if that will make them stop. The husband has his friends over at night. They drink and gamble and argue. The disagreements escalate into angry shouting that invades the floor above and disturbs our sleep. Once, very late, the woman banged on our door, asked to spend the night. Her husband was drunk and had beaten her. Maman hesitated, then let her take my cot. I crept in beside Edith.

Upstairs lives Fräulein Schulmeister. She rents out one room to an artist named Botticello (!) who doesn't pay his rent on time. They scream at each other and he calls her a "whore," whatever that means. Fräulein Schulmeister entertains many gentlemen callers. No one tells me the reason for this or explains how she earns her living.

We were almost sent to an internment camp when we arrived in Basel two years ago. Before the order could be carried out, Edith and I were brought to the Children's Hospital with hepatitis. No one was allowed in the room we shared except for a young nun, an older nun, and the pediatrician, Dr. Adler. Our window faced the promenade by the Rhine. Maman and Papa would walk by as often as possible. If we were awake we would wave and wait for them to wave back. As my sister and I improved, we were permitted to go on the little terrace for short periods – which greatly improved "visiting hours" and our spirits.

Occupied with sickness and recovery, Edith and I had no idea what our parents were enduring. Scarcely had the four of us set foot in the new country than the prospect of internment loomed. We two children fell ill. Our parents had to search quickly for a solution.

It was too much for Papa and as a result, he suffered a major seizure. But Maman held on and found people willing to come to our aid. Fellow refugees, together with the Salvation

Army, helped her secure an apartment near the hospital. The neighborhood might be run-down but the location was ideal. And young Dr. Adler, who supervised the treatment of Edith and me, knew exactly how to frighten the authorities. We were highly contagious, he told them, and would remain so for a while – indefinitely. Contact with us was risky, especially in close quarters, like in a camp, where we could infect multitudes.

The authorities relented. By the time we got better, came home and started school, they had devised a less confining way of controlling us. My parents were instructed to report to the main police station in Basel every Saturday morning. They still had to do this, and were obliged to continue as long as we were in Switzerland.

Keeping our family out of a detention camp was only part of Dr. Adler's plan. He also intended to provide the ongoing care Edith and I would need after we were discharged. For many months we returned to the hospital's outpatient clinic for checkups and tests. Under the doctor's attentive eye we slowly regained our strength.

The center of our world is the *Sommerkasino*. Its name means "summer casino," as it sounds, but the place has nothing to do with summer or casinos, at least since I've known it. It's a large building in a park of trees and lawns. It contains offices and workrooms, a kitchen and a big dining hall which doubles as a theater when the members put on talent shows.

We have a lot of talent here – actors, singers, musicians.

The *Sommerkasino* and its programs are funded by the Jewish community of Basel with help from the Salvation Army. (I'd never heard of this Christian organization, which extended its hand with no conditions and certainly didn't attempt to convert anyone.) There undoubtedly were other contributors, but I don't know enough to say. We are the only recent refugees. The others came in 1939, mostly from Vienna, some from Hungary. This is the meeting ground, self-help association, the work and activity hub of all the Jewish refugees in the city. There's something for everyone.

We come from Monday to Friday. The adults have jobs like carpentry, sewing, repairing shoes, cooking. They are paid in cash, allowing them to afford their rent and a few necessities. Some basics, like clothing and meals during the week, are supplied by the *Kasino*. According to rules laid out by the Swiss government, no refugees may be employed except within our closed organization.

Children as young as four all the way up to young adults of eighteen form a separate community known as the *Kinderhort*. Lore Jacobson is in command, responsible for order and regulation. We think of her as a stern "old maid." Older kids arrive when classes break at noon. We go to various schools – the *Maedchengymnasium* is the elite one – but meet here for lunch until we have to go back. The little ones not yet in first grade have counselors – also refugees – who do crafts with them, play games and keep them busy. Late in the day, when school lets out, the rest of us return.

194

We do homework, often acting as tutors for each other. Some of us need help with math problems. Or we take turns listening and reciting as we memorize poems, history dates and vocabulary in new languages. When the homework burden is light we play catch and soccer. We climb trees and tease each other. In bad weather we are given woodworking tools, raffia, yarns, paper and other art supplies. I've made friends – Edith Korany, Renate Steinitz, Tezie Kanarek – all girls my age and of course, Walter Fischer. My sister, too, has found friends among the children in her age group.

Edith and I are growing rapidly. We didn't bring much to wear from France. The *Sommerkasino* has a big room where the unwanted clothes of Basel's citizens have landed: skirts, sweaters, underwear, socks, dresses and more. Maman takes us there. We are greeted with tact. The people who manage this branch of the *Kasino* are careful not to embarrass us about our needs, and we need everything. The primary consideration is fit. Adults make the decisions. (No one asks children what color and style they prefer.) Since we are the recent arrivals and people know what we went through to get here, they spoil us a bit. When fresh donations come in, the lady in charge tips off Maman.

"Frau Kann," she says, "I think we have some things that will fit the children."

School is conducted in German in this German-speaking part of Switzerland. My friends at the *Kinderhort* know the language. They came here mostly from Austria, so German is their native tongue. For me, attending the *Maedchengymnasium* is a challenging transition. I understood and spoke German when I came, but couldn't write it. I can now, but struggle to master the difficult, highly inflected grammar. Papa has hired an unemployed Viennese lawyer – a stickler for grammar – to tutor me.

My teachers are patient. I know they're pleased with my progress. Besides German, we're beginning to study English and Latin. The grammar lessons I get at home don't do much for my German but are preparing me really well for the Latin.

My art teacher is particularly kind. He proved it when a class trip to the Jura was planned. Worried that the cost would keep me from participating, he walked to our apartment, a considerable distance, and pleaded with my parents to encourage me to come along. (This was during the school day when he knew I was not at home.) There wouldn't be any expense to us, he promised, but nobody need be told.

The Jura Mountains are north of the Alps, lower and older, their rocky peaks rounded by time. In a vanished geologic age, an ocean covered them, leaving layers of sediment as it withdrew.

I swam in a lake surrounded by pasture. The water was clear but reddish from the peat that formed its basin. Blue-splashed clouds overhead became spots of purple reflection. I looked at my body beneath the ripples. The lake had changed its color to reddish brown, a tan I never could achieve in the sun.

I found fossilized shells and snails. One snail was large and heavy. I hauled it into my knapsack, adding it to the collection I would take home. On this day I learned, and won't soon forget, the meaning of the word "Jurassic."

The landscape had its own personality which can be summed up in a word: green. Mosses grew near the lake, encouraged by damp soil. Beyond the meadow stood a pine forest of dark trunks and green needle leaves and between the trees and the water spread a field of grass and small and unspectacular flowers. What I remember is the grass – soft, sappy, full of life, fresh and deliciously fragrant. It was actually a variety of grasses. Most of the blades were tall, except for parts nibbled down by animals. And all of it was green, except for the shadows, which were purple or maroon.

Cows or horses would be lucky to graze here, I thought. The cows and calves I observed did look content. But the horses astonished me – free-roaming mares and foals. I knew nothing about them. Probably they weren't wild, though they seemed so to me. I watched as they ambled and romped and imagined spirited, untamed creatures that would never wear a bridle or heed a master.

I have no special friends at school but I'm accepted by my classmates. Only once was I reminded of being different in not the best way. We were dressing after gym when a girl commented on my undershirt: "That was mine – I outgrew it. My mother gave it to the Red Cross." I felt the color rise in my face. She didn't have to make an announcement.

Papa could have sent me to the *lycée* in Basel. I would have been happy to go but he was adamant – no French school. Definitely not a school run by the government of Maréchal Pétain.

My parents manage not to blame France for our troubles. Not aloud. Not to me. They don't spoil what I remember about a time of chalk and slates, aprons and purple ink, and my first artwork, the crayon heart filled with crayon flowers. *Les marguerites, les coquelicots, les bleuets.*

In those years I learned the history, recited the poems, skipped to the folk dances and sang the Marseillaise, the stirring anthem of the country I believed was mine. Did this same country reject my family, portray us as villains and troublemakers and turn us into exiles?

The wrongs must come from outside, my parents say, from the Nazis. Or if inside, from a small group of collaborators. It helps me that I'm permitted to think this. For the truth is, I still love France.

I don't forget the language. My father and I keep it going. Maman has slipped back into German. Edith, also, has adapted easily to the new linguistic environment. Growing up, she'd been too sick to stray far from home and only acquired French in first grade. Now, even reading and writing in German aren't giving her problems. Edith has a gift for languages. She already speaks like a Basler.

But Papa and I are bonding through French, especially on

long Sabbath walks. Often I sense people's eyes on us. Is it the language or that my father drags his leg, holds his arm rigid? Either way, we don't care. Absorbed in our conversation, we sail from topic to topic. We talk about everything. I always consider Papa the most elegant father a girl could have. Others might notice his leg at first, but if they keep looking they'll see the ramrod posture, the distinguished manner, the intelligent features. They'll see the jaunty way he carries his cane, like a *boulevardier*, a man about town. Bearing no handicap at all, he'd attract attention.

I feel Papa's pride in me. We reinforce each other, create between us an enviable little world. Everyone around us speaks German in the accents of Basel. It sounds rough, not like the *Hoch Deutsch* (High German) I learn in school, and even that can't compare to French. I've decided that French dogs and cats produce more refined barks and meows than their Basel-based counterparts. The thought, which I won't be sharing with my Swiss classmates, brings a smile.

They try, at the *Sommerkasino*, to match the right person with the right job. At first my mother worked in the laundry. Using washboards, the women laundered the clothes of the men in the camps set up for refugees after too many got over the border. (Our family was supposed to be in such a camp.) Maman had to stand, scrubbing dirty socks, shirts and underwear. The hours were long. Then she came home to more chores. This schedule proved strenuous for someone anemic from heavy monthly bleeding. She was transferred to the sewing room.

Here they also work on clothes for men in the camps, but at least she doesn't have to stand and scrub. Instead, she darns socks, sews on buttons, turns collars on shirts that are frayed. Finally she is slated for an operation that will remove the cause of the excessive bleeding – large fibroid tumors that have grown over time.

Most of the men at the *Sommerkasino* work with their hands. Except for a few doctors and lawyers they are carpenters, painters, cooks, shoemakers, upholsterers, tailors. Papa didn't fit in. To remedy this someone came up with what was thought to be the perfect activity for him. A centrally located area, between the shoe repair shop, the dining hall, the sewing room and the *Kinderhort*, was outfitted with tables and chairs, newspapers, magazines, books and a radio. Papa would be in charge of this newly created space, to be known as the "reading room," where people could go to take a break from work.

My father recognized from the start that few of the patrons of his recently acquired little empire would take him seriously. They would come to gossip, smoke, discuss the latest news of the war, maybe leaf through a magazine, and leave. The magazine would be dropped on the floor, the chairs left as they had been moved, the cigarette butts in (or more likely near) the ashtrays.

Papa's attempts to create a neat, appealing library were met with total indifference, but he controlled his temper. He approached a fellow from the shoe repair shop, and in his friendliest, most relaxed manner, said, "Listen, how about putting the magazine back on the shelf where you found it?"

"That's your job. You are paid to do that. I have to get back to work."

Papa now understood exactly how he was regarded. Soon Maman was equally aware. The reading room would have to function without my father's supervision. A routine designed to enhance his sense of purpose and give him a respected place in the community had done quite the opposite. For him it was a setback, and it left him with an aftertaste of futility and despair.

Papa struggles with this state of mind as my mother prepares for major surgery. Maman's operation is timed to coincide with a four-week trip planned for the *Kinderhort* children and teens. (Teens will be girls only.) School is out. Maman spends her days in the sewing room. Papa, having freed himself from the position of undervalued "librarian," is at home. Edith and I are about five days from our vacation and opt to keep him company. We don't have to. He manages alone when we're in school and could continue to do so until Maman returns at suppertime. But we want to help, and he likes the idea of having his girls near, to make life easier and brighter.

Though Edith and I grew up aware our father had extra needs, we don't realize how little he's been doing for himself, and when he goes it alone, how extraordinary are the maneuvers each task requires. Now we pay attention. We are shocked by the details of living that challenge him: tying a shoe, cutting a slice of bread and spreading the butter on it. He puts on a tie, pulling and wrapping with one hand, the other end of the cloth between his teeth. I watch him write. He places a heavy object on the page since he can't secure it with his left hand. The task of opening or closing a door is far from routine when his only good hand is holding a cane. Striking a match to light a cigarette takes a special effort.

Of course, I'm not observing Papa for the first time. But with Maman directing the show, it's amazing how much slipped by me. She has turned caring for him into a high art form, so we don't notice and he never feels incompetent or slighted. I admit I've seen her worn out or short with him, but rarely. When that happens, when they've had words, she will inevitably reverse her position and forgive him. Realizing Edith and I are within range, she will take up his defense. "Just imagine going through life with such an impediment," is a phrase we are used to hearing.

I try to fill in for Maman. At lunch I cut his meat because I know she does that. I also take over her job of slicing the bread. After almost chopping my finger off, I get the hang of it. Papa continues to be self-reliant in matters he has perfected. He dresses with precision. Wearing a belt is impossible, so his trousers are made with suspenders already attached. He is orderly by nature, and fluffs the pillows on the couch and clears the table one plate at a time. But I begin to see that with us around, he asks Edith and me to do things I think he can very well do for himself.

Papa likes soup and fried eggs. I don't mind the preparation but I wonder why it hasn't occurred to him that you can crack an egg with one hand. I try it and prove that it works. He can't wash dishes or cook but why can't he ladle the soup if I hold the bowl? I offer him the chance but he won't accept it.

I should be sympathetic. He worries about Maman, which I understand. We're all worried. He is also depressed, which I don't recognize and can't begin to understand. I only see my father, who, after many years, hasn't learned to do more for himself. He could if he practiced. Maman, I think, has spoiled him.

I'm not proud of being impatient. I'm upset with myself and confused. I'm thirteen and a half years old and unaccustomed to the critical thoughts I harbor. Carrying ungenerous, contradictory feelings about someone I love and want to keep respecting makes me even more unsettled. My irritable mood leaks out. Before I can stop it, a word related to "lazy" escapes my mouth. I see the hurt in Papa's eyes and am immediately ashamed, but I say nothing.

Maman entered the hospital yesterday, leaving Papa in charge. This morning I made breakfast. Edith and I straightened the beds and checked our luggage for items we might have forgotten. Papa walked us to the railway station, insisting on carrying Edith's bag.

We wait on the platform. Our counselors stand ready to take over. The city of Basel has arranged this summer gift for the children of the *Kinderhort* – a month in the Alps! The parents hover, a little anxious. Does my child have what he needs? Will she be homesick? Papa is more than a little anxious. He frets about Maman in the hospital and about us, and probably about himself, soon to be alone in the apartment. Frau Lande, a neighbor Maman has helped in the past, will be looking in on him, seeing that he gets supper. Not that he likes accepting assistance from strangers. I can't say I'm giving any of this a lot of thought, but I am worried about Maman. Her surgery sounds serious. Above all, I'm excited about the trip – seeing the Alps and being the big sister for Edith.

Papa is speaking. I barely hear him in the clamor and confusion: parents imparting last minute advice, young children having second thoughts about leaving, porters shouting over the train whistles. Papa is telling me something about keeping an eye on Edith but I'm not sure. I say something. It must have been a wrong choice of words. I didn't mean to be rude. I have no idea what Papa understood but it wasn't what I had in mind.

From nowhere I register a stinging blow to the side of my face. What ... why? Papa has slapped me in front of everyone. I cover my face with my hands. My cheek burns. I am stunned, then filled with anger. I have never been angry like this. How could my own Papa humiliate me? Edith my sister and Edith my friend and other would-be consolers try to comfort me. I'll never forgive him, ever. A tear slides through my fingers to my wrist. A sob sticks in my throat.

I board the train without saying goodbye, without looking at him or anyone. I don't watch as we pull away. But later I can't help but become engrossed in the landscape. As we leave Canton Basel and travel across the countryside, the hills and fields calm me, gradually erasing my sorrows. I am forced to let them go. Before long, a distant snow-covered outline appears. The Alps are even more beautiful than I imagined.

We step onto the platform. The air is crisp, and mountains rise in every direction. We gather our belongings. Each of us has a knapsack and some sort of suitcase. We put on the knapsacks while the rest of the luggage is loaded onto a horse-drawn cart. Several of the smaller children climb up for a ride to the chalet as the others follow Lore Jacobson away from the station, through the town to where the forest starts.

 Some of the trees are birches, but most are pine, and their scent fills the air. We walk on a rocky path edged with grass and patches of moss, fern and giant wild rhubarb. In the quiet, every sound counts – birdsong, a breaking branch and always, a faint, continuous rushing. As we move into the deeper woods, it grows dark.

We talk less and less, first out of awe, then, as the trail gets steeper, to save energy. We perspire and our backpacks are unaccountably heavy. Lore explains, "We're at a much higher altitude, so there is less oxygen in the air. Now you may feel tired but soon you'll get used to it."

The rushing noise travels with us, more distinct as the space between the trees increases and greater light penetrates. We see the clearing. A meadow opens, huge and green, spread with wildflowers. The mountains that surround us seem closer. We're half convinced we can touch them, make contact after, at most, a short run. Only the crystalline air diminishes the distance. The Alps will fool us again and again in exactly this way.

To the right is our chalet, the *Schieferhaus*, its name inscribed above the terrace. Near it we discover the source of the sound that has accompanied us – a brook speeding over large, shimmering stones, its waters so pure that you can see the grains of sand on the bottom. I drop my knapsack, dip my hands and wrists into the icy stream and splash my face.

The comfortable *Schieferhaus* was built as a ski lodge, though in summer there are no skiers and no snow. Or almost no snow. On hikes we encounter patches of it, remnants of winter on slopes that see more shadow than sun.

Walks and hikes are the main activity of this vacation. Our longest treks take us high, near the snow that never melts. We also visit farmers and taste milk warm from the cow. We begin to identify the wildflowers. They start on the meadow near the chalet – daisies and violets, buttercups and ranunculae, or Persian buttercups, whose heads of closely set yellow-orange petals contrast with the sky, and the small, fragrant, brown *Männertreu*, a word that means "man's faithfulness."

Beside the brook the ground is moist. Tall grasses shade the forget-me-nots and the little purple and yellow pansies and more violets. On the higher meadow we find gentians and yellow arnica and rhododendron bushes with dark pink flowers. Much farther up, where the soil is rocky, are

Katzenpfötchen – "little cat's paws." They are whitish gray and resemble the famous edelweiss, which also grows on the high slopes. The edelweiss symbolizes the Alps, but is rare. I'm on the lookout for these small, furry white flowers, but am disappointed not to discover any.

I gather flowers each day. With some I make bouquets for the dining table. Others I press between sheets of blotting paper and plywood.

At suppertime a meal of Swiss cheese, potatoes and bread and butter, enjoyed in happy company, is a feast.

The night sky reveals more stars than I have ever seen. Stars without end. They seem within reach – almost, like the mountains. The sound of our little brook is ever-present, when I go to sleep, and when I wake up. We wash our clothes in the brook. For my sister, doing laundry is fun. I let her do mine.

By midweek I'm thinking of Maman. She loves flowers. I put together a large bouquet of rhododendron, arnica, daisies, ranunculae and forget-me-nots, wrap it in a piece of damp clothing, and put the whole thing in a box. I get permission to go to the post office in town, which is an hour's walk each way. I imagine Maman's face when she opens the bundle.

I mail Papa a postcard. Staying angry into the distant future was never a real option. He must be terribly lonely by himself. Here, far from everything, I have space to see more clearly – his helplessness, his efforts to be strong, his days filled with obstacles that, to others, are details hardly worth a thought.

We're home. Maman greets us. Her operation and our holiday have both been successful. She's had a hysterectomy. I don't know what this is, but the way Frau Lande talks about it, our concern was justified. We all help – shopping, straightening, cleaning, picking up meals at the *Sommerkasino*.

My mother and I are alone in the apartment. She is lying down, though not asleep. "Renée," she says, "sit beside me." She makes room and I plant myself on the edge of the bed. "It's good to have you by me again." She hesitates as if testing words in her mind before choosing the direct path.

"Papa told me what happened."

I should have expected this. "I'm over it," I say.

She sighs. "You know it's hard for him."

"Yes," I nod.

"After you left for the mountains, Papa came home. He realized what he had done and was deeply upset. Later Frau Lande found him on the sofa. He'd had a seizure."

"Oh!"

"Listen," says Maman. "When your father was twenty he was beginning his apprenticeship. He was athletic and confident – a lot like you. Then came the war and ..."

"I know, Maman."

"Yes, but try and realize it. In a horrible moment so much was taken away. It felt like everything. Of course he had to get well enough to be aware of it. And when he did he suffered a sadness far worse than the physical problems. Imagine, one moment you are young and strong and capable and suddenly it's gone. You consider the years ahead, believing this is how you'll always be. He looked in the mirror and saw … a cripple." The word was taboo in our home. Never had I heard it from either of my parents.

"No!" I say.

"Well, Papa is stubborn."

"I guess that's where Edith gets it."

Maman smiles. "Stubbornness can be a good thing. Papa discovered he had it in him to start a business and build it up. He was a successful man when I met him, with employees who adored and respected him. I fell in love not because he'd made money and could provide for a family – though that never hurts – but because I knew what he'd overcome. And for other reasons, as any young girl. So much has happened. Here we are in this place and we must be grateful. But Papa is without his business and he worries how we'll manage …"

"We'll manage," I say, and mean it.

"He can't believe he is reduced to being – he says – of no real use. He told me he feels again, for the first time since his lowest days, like a …"

"Don't say it." My eyes fill with tears. I get up.

"Wait," says Maman. "Until very recently he had a bright spot to hold on to."

"What?"

"Who, you mean. You. He is enormously proud of you."

"And Edith," I remind her.

"Yes, Edith. He loves both of you. He's proud of both of you. But he knows Edith has a hard road in front of her. He feels concern about her future. But you – you, Renée, have shown, over and over, an ability to face the world, adjust to changes – and there have been a few! You're his red-haired Gypsy. And such a good heart, and such a student!" I lower my eyes. I know my parents are proud of me but they don't generally heap praises. Not so specifically. "Papa thought you and he were getting closer. It kept him going. Now he's afraid he's damaged his relationship with you, that it will not be again what it was. I'm not sure he can bear that."

I feel stricken. "Maman," I say, "it wasn't only him … well, maybe at the train station … but before, when you were away, it was me too. I wasn't patient. I didn't realize how much help he would need. I … I … said an unkind thing."

Maman is quiet. She takes my hand in hers.

◊ ◊ ◊

The linden trees have turned yellow and have begun to

shed their heart-shaped leaves. The smell of wet leaves is in the air. Sometimes on my way to school when I cross the Wettsteinbruecke, the Muenster is hidden in fog.

Papa and I walk along the Rhine quay. The fallen leaves make a slippery carpet under our feet. I stay on Papa's right side, his strong side, so he can hold onto my arm in case he starts to skid. I'm reciting a poem I've been assigned to memorize. Papa surprises me by joining in, having learned the same verses when he was a student, at a time when German was a language of great writers, philosophers, musicians and artists. When it was, at least, free of unpleasant associations. I stop and let him continue. He finishes without a mistake.

We're crossing the old stone bridge. It widens at one point to make space for an enclosure perfect for river gazing. I've had an idea for a while which I confide to no one. I imagine Hitler imprisoned and on display in this structure, to be mocked, shamed, disdained, spat upon by all who go by. Forcing him into the role of unwilling sideshow seems appropriate punishment to me – and severe, given my own horror of humiliation. Like most of the world, I am ignorant of the magnitude of the Nazi evil. My notion of justice will prove vastly unequal to the crime.

News from the front improves. The adults follow developments on the radio and in the papers. Soon the children become aware of the good reports. All of us at the *Sommerkasino* are affected. We dare to hope the tide has turned and our side will win. A hint of elation enters the spirit of our community. Then in December – a setback. Hitler's army has staged a powerful counterattack in the Ardennes Forest in Belgium. The Allies weren't expecting it and lose men in huge numbers. Papa is glued to the radio, taking in the hourly bulletins.

I try to read the faces of the people I see in the streets. How do they feel about these events? Do they want the Allies to win or, in this German-speaking sector, would they prefer a German victory?

The Americans, led by General Patton, reach the Ardennes and halt the Germans in their tracks. It takes two weeks and thousands of lives but the threat is repulsed. Germany has failed to make a comeback. What will be known as the Battle of the Bulge is over and a weight is lifted from our hearts. I look at the pedestrians for signs of joy and relief, but their faces are passive.

The radio brings more good news – General Patton's thrust into Lorraine, particularly toward and into the beautiful city of Nancy. It's easy to identify with what's happening. We lived in the province of Lorraine.

Then, frustration. Patton is stopped. They've run out of fuel. General Eisenhower is allocating the available supplies to Montgomery's soldiers in Holland. But soon we hear reassuring reports. Patton's troops are advancing again from Sarreguemines – our French hometown! They cross into Germany. The river that separates the two countries is the Sarre, Saar in German.

Who are these wonderful soldiers and generals? We call them the *"Amis,"* short for Americans. Their dedication and sacrifice escape no one. It can't be accidental that the word also means "friends." We hear about the Free French under Général Charles de Gaulle. But the real work of liberating Europe is being done by foreigners who have come from half a world away.

◊ ◊ ◊

We refugees aren't in a state of unmixed optimism. Even when Hitler is defeated – and we're saying *when,* not *if* – a fearful accounting remains. What has happened to friends and family left behind? The answer becomes ever clearer, though no one wants to face it.

My parents sit at the table. They are making a list of disappeared loved ones, starting with Opa, going on to Papa's sister Gusta and her husband, Ernst, Onkel Otto, Tante Paula, Tante Marthe, Tante Grete, Cousin Ilse. More than forty names.

Concentration camps are real to us. The KZs. Now we learn two words that grip us like a new nightmare: gas chamber. Every refugee in Basel has family members in a KZ somewhere.

Nineteen forty-four becomes nineteen forty-five. Few adults at the *Sommerkasino* have doubts about the true purpose of Hitler's camps. A year ago we received a postcard from Opa, and several months later, another one. (We had let the Red Cross know we'd made it to Basel, and they enabled an

213

exchange of mail.) Opa's cards say he is well. In the second card he claimed, "My favorite wine still tastes wonderful."

A strange remark. I remember my mother's effort to explain it.

"Opa lets nothing squelch his *joie de vivre*. And," she added, "his dry sense of humor." The cards were preprinted with open spaces for Opa to complete. He's in a place called Terezin. At least he was when he wrote to us.

There is a haven where I put aside worries and fears and all the ordinary thoughts that crowd my head. I stop there after school if I have time, or go there on a Saturday, crossing the river. I don't bring Papa. This section of Gross Basel is too hilly for him, and he probably wouldn't be keen on my love for a Christian building.

The Muenster is never empty but there won't be more than a few people inside. They pray or walk quietly, each one alone. No one intrudes. I notice the scent of candles and the dampness. Sometimes there are fresh flowers. The light filtering through stained glass windows varies according to the weather. Usually it's soft and gentle. There aren't many truly bright days in Basel.

I stare at the pieces of thick colored glass surrounded by frames of black lead, jewel-like fragments that combine to tell a story. Most of the stories are from the New Testament and are unfamiliar. I recognize images from the Bible I know: Moses with the Tablets of the Law, King David with his harp. The characters, the lessons they teach, aren't what fascinate me. My eyes are held by the shapes and colors and the otherworldly light. On rare sunny days it comes through almost like a rainbow.

An organist practices on Saturday afternoons, making the whole space resonate with rich chords and scales that span a great range. When he prepares for a concert I can listen for hours. The high ceiling is a natural amplifier. Sometimes the sounds are especially deep and intense. I touch a stone column and feel it vibrate.

At the back of the building on either side of the altar are doors so low even I have to duck. Each opens to a winding staircase. I can climb as far as I want, up into one of the two towers. The stone steps are worn in the middle. They narrow as they reach the top, where bells ring on the quarter hour. Small windows let in a little light. I look down to the city and river and beyond.

The best part of the Muenster, the part I've made my own, is the cloister, which is seldom visited. I enter through a door off the right aisle or from outside. (It also exits onto a terrace, called the *Pfalz*, which faces the Rhine.)

I walk along the colonnade, breathing the fresh air and feeling the flat stones beneath my feet. Some have inscriptions marking ancient graves. On the wall are bronze plaques, more tombstones from the sixteenth century. Many letters are worn away but I can decipher bits of the Latin, which I'm beginning to study in school.

A fountain in the courtyard breaks the hush. Around it are a few simple rosebushes. I recognize the five-petalled wild rose, which appears in so much of the red sandstone ornament of the cathedral. I close my eyes to imagine the monks and nuns who prayed and meditated here long ago, before the church switched to a Protestant allegiance. I think, with envy, of their solitude, calm, and perfect devotion. No need to worry about grades, clothes, friends. No major decisions to make.

I don't know a lot about Catholic beliefs but I'm impressed that followers are still offered the choice of living apart, of not having to find a job or a mate or raise children or save money or buy and sell. And so be free to walk for days and years along a colonnade in a place of beauty and silence like this.

A piece of red sandstone has broken loose from a corner. I pick it up and wrap it in a handkerchief.

It's February. There's no getting to school without crossing the Wettsteinbrucke, braving the wind and cold, and the icy vapors that ascend from the Rhine. My woolen outer-clothes are warm, but under them, a skirt and knee socks offer little protection. My bare legs freeze and chafe. The river, black and murky, seems the source of all that is damp, penetrating and chill. The dark heart of winter in Basel.

The cold isn't actually extreme. No one can skate on the Rhine, which flows freely. Boats pass through. Humidity and wind give the season its bitter edge. Shivery as I am in socks, only the worst conditions force me into ugly, knitted, bulky and unflattering stockings held up by clumsy garters.

But March is on its way. By the end of that month, days are mild. By the start of April the first flowers appear. I see them under trees and bushes. They burst through the sleepy soil and dress up patches of grass and peek through dead leaves. Small, bright violets.

There are some very different strangers in town, usually clustering in groups of four, five, six. They are young men in uniform, wearing high boots that make them look taller than they already are. The boots emphasize their slender ankles and long legs. They walk with an easy swagger and are friendly, eager to speak with anybody. I like it that these American soldiers are open. They show their feelings. I contrast this with the closed and wary non-expressions on so many Swiss faces. The soldiers speak English, I think. It doesn't sound like the language we're learning. It's softer. But then, they are speaking fast, the syllables running together. I eavesdrop and isolate individual words. How much better to try and have a conversation. I am fourteen years old and eager to test my new skills. A first encounter startles me.

"Hey, Red!"

I hesitate, and then realize he means me. And the remark doesn't sound like an insult. No, having red hair is good. I smile and blush. How different from the French *rouquine* or *poils de carotte* or the German *Rotfuchs*. I say, "Good morning, how are you?"

He replies with a torrent of words, none of them understandable, but I can tell that he is encouraging. He tries again, this time louder. Several intrigued soldiers join us.

I ask, "Are you Americans?"

"Sure are," replies the original soldier, and launches into another presentation. Names of states – a long list I've never heard. America is a country. Where do all these states come from? The only one I know is Texas. I simply hadn't thought of America as a series of strange sounding states. What to say? I reach for a family connection.

"My uncle lives in Pittsburgh."

"Yeah, that's in Pennsylvania. Hank, he comes from Pennsylvania."

I am fascinated with Doug, who comes from Indiana. That must be where Indians live. And there is this other fellow, Jeff, from Buffalo. Is this the place, I ask myself, where buffalo roam? Other young men hail from states filled with *s's* – Mississippi and Massachusetts. One is from the state of New York. But I thought that was a big city.

I can't explain where I'm from. It's too complicated. Although the soldiers have fought in Europe, they aren't deeply acquainted with our geography or history. After a while, I'm comfortable enough to say, "Basel is a beautiful town. I can show you. Yes?"

I, too, am a stranger in the city but have learned to love it – the river, the medieval sections, the elegant Renaissance quarters, the museums, fountains, and, of course, the Muenster. Now I want to share it. Yes?

218

"Sure, okay." What "okay" means I do not ask. It sounds like an agreement.

Since this meeting takes place on the promenade along the Rhine, it's easy to point to the twin spires of the Muenster.

"That is a very old building, the Basel Muenster. Come, I shall show you."

My brief, unexpected career as an impromptu volunteer tour guide begins. The young men have no previous appreciation of Gothic architecture or seventeenth century buildings, but my enthusiasm ignites an interest.

Later we try to sort out a minor confusion about the denomination of the cathedral. "It is Protestant," I say.

"Okay, not Catholic. Lutheran, Presbyterian, Baptist, Episcopalian?" he replies. "What is it?"

We finally understand, on both sides, that this is an area of difference. Here, a Christian who is not a Catholic is a Protestant. That's all.

In early spring a light coat over a cotton dress is sufficient. On wet days, add an umbrella. Walter Fischer is beside me, tall and grown-up despite the knickers and high socks that complete his shirt and jacket.

On another outing not long before, we met at the cinema. We saw *"The Wizard of Oz,"* the first non-cartoon movie in color for either of us.

"What was your favorite part?" Walter had asked afterwards.

"The scene in the poppy fields," I replied.

"The poppy fields! All they did was sleep!"

I explained that it wasn't the sleeping characters that enthralled me but the huge field and countless poppies. He still didn't get it. I reversed the question.

Walter's choice was the part where the tornado carries Dorothy, Toto, the house and more to Oz. The scene had confused me. I'd never heard of a storm this fierce or witnessed any brand of bad weather remotely like it. I tried to pick up what I could from Walter without letting on that I didn't know what a tornado was. They had also called it a "twister" in the black-and-white portion of the movie. I was convinced it was part of the dream sequence. Make-believe, like Oz itself.

There had been drizzle when we left the theater. By this time the rain was steady. I opened my umbrella and invited Walter to come under it. He wasn't about to move in close even to stay dry.

"No, no, no," he said. "I don't need it." I repeated my offer but he stuck to his decision. Shoulders hunched against the elements, he trod on. I stole sidelong glances as rain soaked his dark hair, ran down his high cheekbones, dropped from his eyelashes, and drenched his clothes.

Today it is raining again and Walter is prepared. He raises a large black umbrella. He could invite me to share it. It would be so easy! I keep hoping he won't waste the afternoon's romantic possibilities, because the city is beautiful in the April rain. The river and buildings are silvery. The droplets of water catch any available light and make it more intense. Maybe Walter will reach over and slip my arm through his, like the couples I see. We'll walk close together under the dripping linden trees. I send him this message via telepathy, but am unsuccessful. Walter is content with the world as it is. I put up my own umbrella. My small one and his large one occupy the space between us. We're farther apart than ever.

My informal tours are going smoothly. I gain confidence. It's not hard to gather a few curious young Americans willing to walk in Basel's ancient section. We always end up at the Muenster, my intended focus. I specialize.

We enter the building and admire the windows. We walk in the cloister and enjoy the fountain. Back inside, I open the door to the narrow stone steps, warning my companions to duck. We climb the steep, long, winding staircase. Since I'm wearing a dress I make them go ahead of me.

We're out of breath at the top. What a view! We can see France and Germany and – the weather's clear – all the way to the Black Forest. If we're lucky, we'll be up here when the bell is rung. A bonus.

"The cathedral is a thousand years old," I tell the soldiers. "There was an earthquake in the 1300s and it had to be rebuilt."

My friends are impressed. They barely grasp that this building was already old when their country was "discovered" by Christopher Columbus. The Middle Ages and the Renaissance were over when America was added to the maps. For these men, the words "old" and "ancient" indicate very different time frames from mine.

I'm getting used to hearing Americans speak. They don't say "Good morning," but "Hi." Not "Goodbye," but "So long," or something that sounds like "Seeya." I've been keeping a small notebook where I ask them to write their names and home addresses. (Sometimes they add their army addresses.) They write "Call me when you get here," or "Call me when you grow up." Or they say it and smile.

Maman and Papa have gone out. Edith and I see an envelope on the table. Any letter is cause for excitement, especially when instead of Monsieur or Madame or Frau, we notice, in bold handwriting, Mademoiselle. We pounce immediately. The word after Mademoiselle turns out to be Renée.

"For me," I say. I rip it open. "It's from Renée Caussidière!" The message isn't long. Words aren't my friend's natural medium.

"What does she say?"

"Her father's in a German work camp. She's alone with her mother. The two of them do a lot of the heavy work her father did around the theater."

"What else?"

"That's the main thing. She asks for Maman and Papa. She really liked Maman."

"Does she mention me?"

"I was coming to that," I say, restraining a smile. "She wants to know if you're still a pain in---." Edith tosses a pillow. I duck. "She said it, not me!"

"And what are you going to write back?"

"I'll say you're no longer quite such a pain but still totally stubborn -" Another pillow misses me. "And a bad shot."

"Fine," says my sister, "and you can ask her if she has any new words for us that can actually be said in public!" Edith is twelve, the age of Renée Caussidière when I first met her.

In the *Sommerkasino* the talk is about where to go when the fighting stops. Everyone says the war will end soon. We're lucky. We'll be returning to Sarreguemines, where Papa had his business, where we had the apartment with all our belongings that we left so suddenly. It seems a lifetime ago. The idea of being in France again excites us, though we don't know what to expect. The Pétain government will be gone. About that we are sure.

Most of the refugees have no clear plans. Many of the younger ones are determined to go to Palestine and help build the land. A few of the older ones speak of returning to Vienna or Budapest. We've all grown to love Basel. Some of the families who came from Vienna like to think they'll be allowed to stay, having been here since 1939.

"They're fooling themselves," Papa says. "They have been temporarily accommodated. Switzerland will never give citizenship rights to anyone not born here. They can't wait for us to leave and don't care where we go."

I believe him. For six years the landlocked Swiss have had to share limited resources. In the streets I've overheard, "Thank goodness the war will be finished and the damn refugees will get out." I sense an undercurrent of anti-Semitism.

The day is coming when we will learn the truth about our relatives. Maman tries to sound hopeful when she speaks of her father, but the sadness and uncertainty in her eyes say what her words will not. Every night I ask God to keep Opa safe and bring him to us. We can't do it so it's up to Him. At the same time I question why He allows cruelty and injustice in the first place. The authority of religion – anybody's religion – is fading for me. Yet I don't neglect my "direct line." Not as long as there's a chance for Opa.

The Germans surrendered this week. On Tuesday they signed the papers in Reims. On Wednesday, in Berlin. That was May 8, 1945 – Victory in Europe Day. But it's only being celebrated now, on Thursday. We're out of school early.

I'm at the Muenster with two soldiers, showing them around. After visiting the nave and the cloister we stand on the terrace. From here we can see the Rhine in both directions. The men are impatient to get back to their units, but I convince them they can't leave without a climb to the top of one of the towers. Both doors are open. We begin our ascent.

It is almost noon, time for the bells. As we near the top I look forward to the twelve melodious tones, but in their place is a series of powerful, vibrating gongs that seem to shake the whole belfry and our insides. This is a bell I have never experienced – slow, repeated, deafening. One ring, a brief pause while the note reverberates, then another. We put our hands over our ears. The intensity of sound, even as we depart from the source, barely lessens.

We come out to the plaza, the Muenster Platz. A crowd has

gathered. People are embracing, shaking hands. These are the same formal Swiss I see every day, men in shirts and ties, women in tailored dresses, skirts and blouses. A few women wear the traditional brown and white costume of Basel.

There is crying and praying. An older woman is in active prayer. The American soldiers are noticed right away. Some of the Swiss greet them with blessings and thanks.

The booming sound continues, loud enough to be heard throughout the city and nearby Baselland. The solemn bell makes it official. The war is really over.

The Peace Bell is still ringing as I cross the Wettsteinbruecke. Through tears I look at the impassive Rhine River, back over my shoulder at the majestic Muenster as if to imprint it in my heart. After crossing the bridge I take the slower way home, along the Rhine Promenade. The linden trees are in full foliage and bloom, and their fragrance envelops me. It is as if the bell's booming waves made the scent more penetrating. Sounds, scents and emotions mingle into an overwhelming experience.

I turn from the Promenade onto the Rheingasse, another turn and I find myself standing before our modest house. For the first time I become aware of the inscription above the front door, *"Zur Linde."* The address is No. 3 Lindenplatz. A linden tree grows in the center of the small square in front of the house.

This city has become a part of me and leaving Basel will be difficult. However, the thought of returning to France outweighs my sadness. I begin to wonder what awaits us.

Epilogue

We had been the last refugees to arrive in Basel. We were the first to leave. Everything happened so quickly that saying goodbyes was not a prolonged affair.

There was not a lot to pack for our journey back to Sarreguemines. We had spent six years running from persecution, and knew there would be nothing left of our former home. After all, Alsace and Lorraine had been occupied by the Germans for the last six years and had borne the brunt of Patton's army as it bulldozed its way to the German border.

The train ride, despite many changes due to damaged rails, did not seem very long. Beautiful Alsace-Lorraine, so verdant with hops, vineyards and gardens, so neat and clean, was devastated. Buildings were in ruins, or at least pockmarked by artillery shells. Few houses had windows left. Streets were torn up, bridges demolished. Disabled tanks, trucks and jeeps were stranded, abandoned.

In Sarreguemines itself, the railroad station had been shelled. Our former apartment building was standing but, of course, our own apartment was occupied. Our friends, the Gilers, had found an apartment slightly away from the town center. They offered to shelter us until we could find something.

Before school started that year, an apartment was found for us. It had some furniture in it and we rented it as was. Not a single window remained intact. It had not been occupied for a while, and large families of mice had made their homes in the dresser drawers.

Edith and I resumed school at the *Ecole Supérieure de Jeunes Filles* and the *Lycée de Sarreguemines* respectively. There was no problem adjusting. Most of our classmates had spent the last six years under German occupation, and their schooling had been in German. Now French was once more the official language. I was thrilled to finally be in a French-speaking environment again and to participate in the preparation for the *baccalauréat*. At the *lycée*, there were four Jewish boys, but I was the only Jewish girl.

The reality of the war was everywhere. Sarreguemines was in ruins. A temporary bridge replaced the old one that had been blown up. The streets had been torn up by the passage of tanks and every building bore evidence of shelling. German prisoners of war marched past our home every morning on their way to clear the surrounding Lorraine countryside of mines their compatriots had planted throughout the region.

Food and supplies were still scarce. We were lucky to be receiving "Care" packages from America, not only from Uncle Nathan's family, but from cousins Lucie and Leon, and even from people we did not know. The parcels contained coffee, sugar, preserves, chocolate, condensed milk, peanut butter, clothing. The clothing, regardless of size, enchanted Edith and me; peanut butter was a new experience for us!

Sarreguemines' synagogue had, of course, been destroyed.

Where it had stood, a wooden barrack served as our temple. Few Jewish families remained. Many had been deported. Some decided to remain in other parts of France or had managed to leave Europe. Only two of the four Jewish boys at my *lycée* were from Sarreguemines; the other two commuted from Diemeringen. We were lucky: our family of four had survived, together. However, a gnawing certainty was beginning to take hold. Our hope of finding Opa and other relatives alive was a chimera. We were alone in Europe.

After a second Seder in Sarreguemines it was Edith who wondered why we could not join our family in America. While this had never been a real thought in my parents' mind before, it made a lot of sense to them and our relatives in America wanted us to join them.

It took very little time to make the necessary preparations, obtain the papers, affidavits, visas, and travel reservations. Once more I was faced with the prospect of leaving France. I was utterly unhappy. Between the Seder and the actual departure, I was kept very busy with preparations for and the actual passing of the *baccalauréat*, both written and oral examinations. My lonely voice of sorrow was of no consequence, and a few weeks after the exam, we were off to Paris to spend a few days with our friends the Epsteins before leaving from Calais for England, where we boarded the SS *Queen Elizabeth*. I was ill with grief throughout the journey and nothing could console me.

On July 17, 1947, my family arrived in New York Harbor on a typical brown, muggy, hot summer day. We were met by family, some I knew, others I met for the first time. Our first week was spent in the Bronx, with visits to other parts of the city. I remember being taken to Radio City Music Hall in Manhattan, on a car ride through Central Park, and to Addie Vallins, an ice cream parlor in the Bronx. Discovering banana splits did a great deal to lift my spirits.

Cousin Leon had taken Uncle Nathan's car, a big Hudson, to come get us. And so we left New York for Pittsburgh, the Steel City. Traveling from the Bronx through New York, New Jersey and Pennsylvania gave me an idea of how vast, rich and beautiful my new country was.

Pittsburgh was different from my expectations. I grew to love the city as my American hometown. It had remained very green despite its smoke-belching steel mills. Many hills and parks gave it special character. There were few high-rising buildings in 1947 and many pleasant neighborhoods, not the least of which, Squirrel Hill, where my father's brother lived.

I was only sixteen, and while the University of Pittsburgh would have accepted me, I chose instead to spend a year at Taylor Allderdice High School. In addition to growing more fluent in English, I learned about American mores and rituals. For the first time in my life I was at a school where Jewish children were a majority. Even some of my teachers were Jewish. I also learned about American football, sororities, fraternities, the American grading system, Sadie Hawkins Day, Halloween. American girls my age "went steady" and "got pinned."

By the time I was admitted to the University of Pittsburgh, I felt at home. I loved the Gothic skyscraper known as the

Tower of Learning (also called the Heights of Ignorance by students at the rival university, Carnegie Tech!). Its beautiful Nationality Rooms and the Heinz Chapel, a copy of the Sainte Chapelle in Paris, fascinated me.

During my first year at Pitt, a few weeks before my eighteenth birthday, I met a young man who was studying architecture at Carnegie Institute of Technology. We shared a love of the arts and he introduced me to many aspects of American culture. It was a *coup de foudre* for me, and after promising my father that I would complete my university studies, Art Silver and I were married when I was nineteen. We began life together in New York City, my husband's hometown.

Love of languages led me first to a position as a translator for a large mining firm. I completed my degree with night courses at Hunter College. A few years after the birth of our son, Marc, I became a New York City language teacher.

For my family the "Hitler Terror" began in 1935 when we had to leave the Saarland. I was four years old. I happily accepted and loved my new country without reservation and never expected to be rejected so brutally.

The summer of 1942 was the hardest part of the war. First the public humiliation in which I was denied the Pétain prize because of my "race." Then weeks of separation from my family while hidden in Le Chambon, weeks of constant fear for my parents' safety.

It was a time when I began to feel inferior because of my race and my national origin. Unable to deal with this, I chose to repress my memories and ignore them. I never spoke about either the school episode or Le Chambon.

When one day in 1989 I read an article in the New York Times about an award-winning film documenting Le Chambon sur Lignon, I informed my husband that I thought this might be about a town where I had spent time during World War II. He accompanied me to see the film at a synagogue in Great Neck, New York.

Weapons of the Spirit was a moving portrayal of spiritual and heroic people who had saved Jewish children under the inspired leadership of Pasteur André Trocmé. One of the individuals brought to life on screen was Madame Madeleine Dreyfus, a social worker who had brought children from Lyon to Le Chambon. When her "little black book" was opened on screen, I screamed and nearly fainted. On one page, my sister's name appeared with our address in Villeurbanne and her date of birth. My name followed.

My scream sharply reawakened a memory, but now the emphasis was not one of shame for me but the realization that, unknowingly, I had been a part of an extraordinary moment in French history. The people of Le Chambon sur Lignon had not just sheltered and saved a few children from Lyon, but nearly 5,000 youngsters from many corners of France. I also understood, finally, that my stay in Le Chambon had, indeed, not been "a vacation in the mountains" for Edith and me but, what I only suspected as a child, a way of saving

232

our lives. During the summer of 1942 mass arrests of foreign Jews for deportation to "points east" were made throughout Occupied and Unoccupied France. My parents, too, were saved by being hidden in a Christian home.

I went back to Le Chambon in 1990 for a reunion. While some of the children saved by the Chambonnais knew each other, I knew no one, having been truly hidden and secluded. With the help of a topographic map, my husband and I were able to find the isolated farmhouse where I was first hidden. It was called "La Souche," and the young Marcel with whom I had herded cows and goats still lived there with his wife and some of his twelve children. None of the other people I had met were either still living in Le Chambon or living at all.

My visit to Le Chambon was highly emotional. It reactivated memories I had hidden from myself for forty-eight years. Now as an adult with a grown son, I truly understood how much danger and responsibility I had faced as an eleven year-old. Unaware of the hatred facing us from the Vichy government I had left my shelter, picked up my little sister and simply left Le Chambon to undertake a complicated return to Lyon, unaccompanied and unannounced. Miraculously I had reached Lyon safely.

At eleven I had been totally oblivious to the risks of such a journey. Now, as an adult, I looked back on the experience with awe and gratitude.

Historical Notes

When we think of France during World War II, we think of a victim of Hitler's conquests, of a country suffering under the boot of the German, forced to endure an occupation and eagerly awaiting liberation. And thus it was for most French men and women. For a significant segment of France, however, this "defeat" was thought of in a strangely different way.

It did not take long after the declaration of war on September 3, 1939 for France to surrender to Germany on June 22, 1940. It took even less time for the Collaborationist Vichy government under the leadership of the aging Maréchal Philippe Pétain to take over. This new government's first laws were aimed at discriminating against Jews. On July 17, 1940, a Ministry to Deal with the Jewish Question was formed. Elements of France were waiting for this opportunity. They openly "preferred Hitler to the Jew Léon Blum," one of the Socialist party leaders and former Premier Ministre (1936).

Even prior to France's defeat there had been a right-wing shift against Bolsheviks, capitalists and Jews, the latter being blamed for the two others. The intellectual Jews, writers, artists, theater people and philosophers were branded as communists while the well-to-do bankers and professionals were labeled as capitalists. Vichy politics encouraged the flowering of fascist elements in France. The newsreels being shown at movie theaters spoke in glowing terms of the brave

German soldiers battling Bolsheviks on the Eastern front; repairing damage to roads and railroads in France, bringing medical services to France; and, starting in 1943, building vast defense systems along the Atlantic coast against the English (and later Anglo-American) "threat." We tend to be familiar with France's hatred of the "*Boches*"[1] but in reality their Anglophobic sentiments were deeper and had begun much earlier.

William the Conqueror was a Norman, and with his victory at Hastings in 1066, began an Anglo-Norman rule of England. Normandy was a part of France, and Norman leaders were vassals of the King of France. From the eleventh to the fifteenth century, parts of France were ruled by Anglo-Normans and fought over with French kings. These ongoing battles became known as the Hundred Years War (1337 to 1453). The final battle was one in which Joan of Arc led French forces. She was eventually captured and handed over to the English forces by the dukes of Burgundy, then British allies. After a trial, she was burned at the stake. Joan of Arc is now the patron saint of France. As history was being taught in the *école élémentaire*, poor Jeanne d'Arc was the victim of the English.

In the eighteenth century, the French helped a young group of overseas colonies achieve independence from the tyranny of England.

---

1 "*Boche*" is the pejorative term used by the French to describe their neighbors, the Germans.

In the nineteenth century, it was the Duke of Wellington who led a victorious British Army at Waterloo, decisively defeating Napoleon's military and ending the Napoleonic era. Empire building and the acquisition of colonies in Asia and Africa created a rivalry between the two nations that lasted well into the twentieth century.

When France capitulated in 1940, Général Charles de Gaulle took a contingent of the French army to England, where it became known as Free France. They fought alongside Allied forces for the remainder of the war and participated in the Normandy Invasion. In 1940, the Pétain régime condemned De Gaulle as a traitor!

The fact that England had been France's ally in both world wars was quickly set aside by the new government. Little by little the enemy was no longer the *Boche*. By 1940 an afternoon at the cinema included newsreels describing the enthusiastic volunteers who joined the German army to take part in their battle against the Bolsheviks. French workers volunteered to go to work in German factories; others were recruited forcefully. For every three workers, one French prisoner of war was to be repatriated. This sounded very promising and efficient but did not reflect the reality. Germany continued to need able bodied men and women to work in the war effort as their own men were in uniform on numerous fronts. French propaganda newsreels showed the wonderful conditions awaiting French workers in Germany, such as good sanitation, housing, medical attention, training opportunities, etc.

The *"actualités"*[2] spoke of a *"Révolution Sociale."* Pétain
was shown meeting Hitler, then Franco. Parades and official
meetings used the raised arm salute with enthusiasm.
Germany was thanked for having given its blood to save
Europe and, "we must help her."

When it came to anti-Semitic laws, no government of an
occupied country collaborated more enthusiastically than the
Pétain Régime. If the Germans had only had the Gestapo to
do their work in France, they could not have done half the
damage. Some of France's decisions regarding the treatment of
Jews were even more cruel than the Nuremberg Laws [3]. Pierre
Laval was a powerful member of the Pétain government. It
was his decision to ignore the Germans' request not to include
children under sixteen in the roundups. Even more cruel
was the decision by the head of the police department, René
Bousquet, to separate these very children from their parents
before sending them on to their death in Auschwitz "in order
to minimize the emotional experience!"

French-made propaganda films appeared comparing Jews to
rats by virtue of proliferation, dirt and undesirability. They
were clearly the cause of France's problems and needed to

---

2 Newsreels seen at movie theaters
3 The Nuremberg Laws of 1935 were anti-Semitic laws in Nazi Germany defining the parameters for being classified a Jew. Under these
  laws, Jews were deprived of their rights of citizenship, and restrictions
  were imposed prohibiting everything from performing in a sym-
  phony orchestra to owning a pet cat. Jews could not exercise professions or attend universities; intermarriage to Aryans, i.e., non-Jews,
  was strictly forbidden. The new laws legalized the persecution and
  eventual deportation and annihilation of the Jewish population of
  Germany.

237

be eliminated. They were kings of the black market and had held key roles in the Socialist government that led to France's defeat. They were depicted in large yellow posters, with huge hooked noses, thick protruding lips, warts, claw-like hands and bulging eyes. A popular movie, *"Le Juif Süss,"* being shown all over France, further illustrated the ugly nature of the *Juif* both physically and morally! While the adjective *"israélite"* had been used to speak of Jews prior to the Vichy Government, the adjective *"juif"* took on a more pejorative meaning, with an emphasis on the final *"f"* sound, making the word a profanity in itself.

THE VEL D'HIV

In June, 1942 the Vichy government decreed that all Jews must wear the yellow star identifying them as *"Juif."* Life became increasingly untenable for all Jews in France, but, of course, particularly for those who did not have French nationality. The Vichy government rationalized that they were protecting French Jews and only cleansing France of foreign Jews. In due time, even naturalized French Jews were in danger. French nationality had to go back over several generations to protect them from deportation. Lawyers were kept busy with the task of determining "who was truly a French Jew." Many were "denaturalized." Even French Jews going back generations were denied higher education, access to the professions and were forbidden attendance at public events.

In Occupied France, Germans made the laws regarding Jews.

June - July 1941 marked a decisive intensification in the "rafles" or massive roundups. Before the German occupation, it would not have been possible to have an organized massive roundup, but in September, 1940 the Germans demanded that Jewish people of the Occupied Zone register with the police. A color-coded filing system classified Jews according to nationality, profession and street address. This efficient file was known as the "fichier Tulard," named for its creator, André Tulard, Head of "Jewish Questions" at the prefecture.

The massive roundup of July 1942 had to be scheduled not to interfere with July 14, Bastille Day. While the French national holiday was not officially celebrated in the Occupied Zone, it was thought best not to risk civil uprisings. Thus on July 16, 1942 a well-organized round-up took place in Paris, starting in the early morning hours. It was a day which subsequently has become a symbol of France's inhumane treatment of Jews. It is known as the *"Rafle du Vel d'Hiv."*

Quickly, before word could get out and anyone escaped, 13,152 Jews were arrested by French policemen. There might have been a reason for picking up the able-bodied men to work in Germany, where their own men were at the front. This did not diminish the French *gendarmes'* zeal, and they also rounded up 5,802 women and 4,051 children under the age of sixteen. The Germans had been explicit in not wanting these very young children.

Some of those arrested were taken to internment camps. The majority came to the *Vel d'Hiv.*

Vel d'Hiv was the popular name for the *Vélodrome d'Hiver*, a covered bicycling track in Paris. Air conditioning had not as yet been invented. The arena had a glass roof which had been painted dark blue to hide any light from enemy (British) bombers. The windows had been screwed shut for security. Five of the ten lavatories were sealed to prevent escape; the other five were blocked. Into this situation some 12,000 were herded on a hot July day. Except for water and food brought in by the Quakers and the Red Cross, there was none.

In this living hell, some prisoners committed suicide and many lost their minds. Those who tried to escape were shot on the spot. After five days the prisoners were taken to several internment camps and then shipped to Auschwitz. Not one child returned.

I have described the *Vel d'Hiv* event because it has come to symbolize France's role in the extermination of Jews. There were numerous internment camps in France. Around Paris we had Drancy, Beaune-la-Rolande and Pithiviers. Opening camps throughout France, Occupied and Unoccupied, created jobs and kept *gendarmeries* busy for the duration of the war. Some of the camps had been established even before the war to receive Spanish refugees after the Spanish Civil War, to control Gypsies, and to imprison communists. The new camps springing up were strictly for Jews. They were internment camps, sort of holding pens, prior to their shipment, via French railroad cars to deportation camps from which they were eventually shipped to "points east" such as Auschwitz, Buchenwald and Maidenek. Here is a partial list of the names of these camps. The names are so lovely that it is hard to imagine them as death portals...

Gurs, St. Cyprien, Rivesaltes, Les Milles, Les Alliers, Avrillé-les-Poinceaux, Le Barcarès, Bourg Lastic, Bram, Brens, Choiseul, Royalieu, Douadic, Fort Barraux, Lalande, Marolles, Masseube, Les Mazures, Mérignac , Mesday-du-Maine, Montceau-les-Mines, Nexom, Noé-Mauzac, Les Tourelles, Port Louis, Récébédou, Camp de Rieucros, Saint-Paul d'Eyjeaux, Saint-Sulpice-la-Pointe...